# in Christ alone

# in Christ alone

LIVING

*the*

GOSPEL

CENTERED

LIFE

# Sinclair B. Ferguson

**℟**

*Reformation Trust*

PUBLISHING

A DIVISION OF LIGONIER MINISTRIES · ORLANDO, FLORIDA

Published by Reformation Trust
A division of Ligonier Ministries
400 Technology Park, Lake Mary, FL 32746

Second printing, April 2008
Printed in the United States of America

Cover design: Geoff Stevens
Interior design and typeset by Katherine Lloyd, The DESK, Sisters, Oregon.

**Library of Congress Cataloging-in-Publication Data**
Ferguson, Sinclair B.
  In Christ alone : living the Gospel-centered life / Sinclair B. Ferguson.
    p. cm.
  ISBN 1-56769-089-0
  1. Christian life--Presbyterian authors. 2. Jesus Christ--Person and offices. I. Title.
  BV4501.3.F467 2007
  248.4--dc22
                                              2007036845

To Libbie,
Alasdair, Rebeckah,
Éowyn, and Alden.
In loving gratitude for Al.

# CONTENTS

# FOREWORD

I t is hard to conceal the sense of pleasure and privilege that accompanies the opportunity to write this foreword. Along with so many, I have found Sinclair Ferguson's writing to be profoundly helpful. It is hard to believe that twenty-seven years have elapsed since I first read *The Christian Life*. I remember as a young pastor being sorely tempted to preach my way through that introduction to Christian doctrine because not only was it comprehensive, it was so wonderfully clear. As I read this manuscript, I found myself employing Ronald Reagan's memorable line in debating Jimmy Carter in 1980: "There you go again!" Sinclair has done it again!

Here is rich theological content distilled with pastoral care and attention so as to make it accessible to every reader. How else could we explain a chapter on Christian liberty that bears the title "Eating Black Pudding"? As you benefit from each of these fifty short chapters, you may feel as if you have enjoyed the privilege of looking over the professor's shoulder at a thumbnail sketch of his lecture notes. Or, better still, that you have sat with your pastor as he has encouraged you to see that, in the words quoted from John Calvin, "salvation whole, its every single part is found in Christ" (p. 7).

It is this emphasis that makes the book so timely. One of the signs of aging is the temptation to view all our yesterdays as the good old days and to find in the present more causes for alarm and disappointment than are justified. As Christians, we are not exempt, and some might argue that we are more prone than others to this perspective. In light of that, I now proceed with caution. Is it wrong to suggest that earlier generations were more thoroughly grounded in the gospel, better versed in the Scriptures, and more convinced that a new life in Christ is lived on the pathway of joyful obedience? How can we possibly tell?

First of all, listen to the present generation talk. I thoroughly enjoy the privilege of addressing students at Christian colleges throughout the country. Their enthusiasm and creativity spur me on, but an accompanying uncertainty and lack of definition in basic Christian doctrine are causes for genuine concern. Some cannot, for example, explain why Mormonism is not Christian because they are unsure of the doctrine of the Trinity. Many appear to be uncertain about the exclusive claims of Jesus, and with the prevailing emphasis on ecology and poverty, many would be hard-pressed to agree with George Smeaton that "to convert one sinner from his way, is an event of greater importance, than the deliverance of a whole kingdom from temporal evil."

Second, consider what is being read by this generation. If the best sellers tell the story, we are preoccupied with imaginative descriptions of end-time phenomena while searching for ways to live up to our human potential. Books on self-improvement and "how-to" texts on all matters earthly sell in abundance. We are reading about our bodies to the neglect of our souls as we measure success by achievement in the "here and now," having lost sight of the "then and there."

Third, hear our loss of focus on the gospel in our songs. This is no comment on musical styles and tastes, but simply an observation about the lyrical content of much that is being sung in churches today. In many cases, congregations unwittingly have begun to sing about themselves and how they are feeling rather than about God and His glory.

What, then, is the antidote to theological vagueness in our students, our books, and our songs? We need to learn to preach the gospel to ourselves because it is the A to Z of Christianity. We need, as chapter 28 makes clear, to be reminded of the three tenses of salvation. All this and more is accomplished by Dr. Ferguson as he consistently turns our gaze to Christ, the author and finisher of our faith.

We are helped in the process by the work of gospel-saturated hymn writers. Over the centuries, Isaac Watts, John Newton, William Cowper, and many others provided the church with biblical theology in memorable melodic form. Today, men such as Keith Getty and Stuart Townend are doing the same with compositions such as their contemporary hymn that shares its title with this book: "In Christ Alone." We should be encouraged by the fact that "In Christ Alone" has become something of an anthem for the church in the first decade of this century. As Alec Motyer has rightly observed,

"When truth gets into a hymnbook, it becomes the confident possession of the whole church." Perhaps all that is necessary to expose the shallowness of our songs and to cause us to praise God as we ought is for pastors and poets and musicians to drink from the same fountain. Then biblical exposition will issue in song and our hymns will be full of the gospel.

It is a double joy to count the author of this book and the writers of this song as my friends, and I can commend both the book and the hymn with gratitude and enthusiasm.

*—Alistair Begg*
Parkside Church
Cleveland, Ohio
September 2007

# PREFACE

I*n Christ Alone*, while small in size, has been long in the writing. Indeed, it has taken two decades to produce. That is not so much because its author is a slow writer but because almost the entire book is a tapestry of articles written over the years for two periodicals, *Eternity Magazine* and *Tabletalk*. Only through a variety of circumstances did it become clear that when sewn together these various pieces would present a picture of the blessings of life in Christ.

As for the various chapters, they began life in the early 1980s when two Christian leaders and mutual friends, the late James Montgomery Boice and R. C. Sproul, befriended me, then a young seminary professor from another land. Over the years, both Jim and R. C. extended to me unfailing kindness and friendship, and the privilege of sharing in their ministries in Philadelphia, Orlando, and other parts of the United States. In addition, both men afforded opportunities to write for the magazines with which they were involved, *Eternity Magazine* in the case of Jim Boice and *Tabletalk* in the case of R. C.

*In Christ Alone* is a small down payment on the debt I owe to these two friends.

I am grateful to the leaders of the Alliance of Confessing Evangelicals for their graciousness in granting permission for the use of several articles from *Eternity Magazine*. These articles, forming several chapters in this volume, are maintained on the Alliance Web site, www.alliancenet.org, as part of its mission of calling the twenty-first-century church to a new reformation and proclaiming the great evangelical truths of the gospel. The Alliance, originally spearheaded by Jim Boice, continues to carry out its mission by broadcasting solid biblical teaching on radio and by sponsoring events such as the Philadelphia Conference on Reformed Theology. I count it a privilege to serve as an Alliance Council member.

I am also grateful to my friends at Ligonier Ministries (www.ligonier.org) and its Reformation Trust Publishing division (www.reformationtrust.com)

for the encouragement and help they have given me to complete this project. Greg Bailey in particular has gone far beyond the call of duty in perfectly balancing personal encouragements to me with his editorial skills in bringing this project to completion, and I am both grateful and indebted to him. Ligonier disseminates R. C.'s teaching in audio and video forms; produces his daily *Renewing Your Mind* radio program; sponsors conferences; and publishes God-honoring books and music as part of its mission of proclaiming the holiness of God. Its daily devotional magazine, *Tabletalk*, is now in its 31st year. The editors were most gracious in granting permission for the use of numerous articles for this volume.

As the conclusion of *In Christ Alone* indicates, these pages came together in my mind just as my longtime friend and colleague Al Groves had gone to be with Christ. It is to his memory that *In Christ Alone* is dedicated. The conclusion not only refers to Al but contains material by him. I am indebted to Libbie Groves and to her family for permission to include that material here. Please read the conclusion last.

It remains only to express my gratitude to Eve Huffman, my secretary at First Presbyterian, Columbia, for her characteristically cheerful efficiency in helping me prepare these pages for publication, and to my longtime friend Alistair Begg for his foreword.

Nothing of much significance happens in my life apart from the devotion, prayerfulness, love, and friendship of my wife, Dorothy. To her and to our family I owe more than words can express or time can repay.

*—Sinclair B. Ferguson*
First Presbyterian Church
Columbia, S.C.
August 2007

# In Christ Alone

*When we see salvation whole,*
*    its every single part*
*        is found in Christ,*
*And so we must beware*
*    lest we derive the smallest drop*
*    from somewhere else.*

*For if we seek salvation, the very name of Jesus*
*    teaches us*
*        that he possesses it.*

*If other Spirit-given gifts are sought—*
*    in his anointing they are found;*
*        strength—in his reign;*
*        and purity—in his conception;*
*        and tenderness—expressed in his nativity,*
*            in which in all respects like us he was,*
*                that he might learn to feel our pain:*

*Redemption when we seek it, is in his passion found;*
*    acquittal—in his condemnation lies;*
*    and freedom from the curse—in his own cross is given.*

*    If satisfaction for our sins we seek—we'll find it in his*
*        sacrifice;*
*    and cleansing in his blood.*
*If reconciliation now we need, for this he entered Hades.*
*    To overcome our sins we need to know*
*        that in his tomb they're laid.*
*Then newness of our life—his resurrection brings*
*    and immortality as well comes also with that gift.*

*And if we also long to find*
  *inheritance in heaven's reign,*
    *his entry there secures it now*
  *with our protection, safety, too, and blessings that abound*
    *—all flowing from his royal throne.*

*The sum of all is this:*
  *For those who seek*
    *this treasure-trove of blessings of all kinds,*
      *in no one else can they be found*
      *than him,*
    *for all are given*
      *in Christ alone.*[1]

—John Calvin

# PART I

# The Word
# Became Flesh

*The Creator took on creatureliness. Thinking about this can be tough going at first, even for Christians. We should not be surprised that this truth staggers our minds. If need be, then, read this section and return to its chapters after reading the rest of the book.*

# PROLOGUE TO CHRIST

The Gospel of John has always been regarded as the most theological of the four Gospels. As John Calvin said, with some insight, "The first three exhibit [Christ's] body, if I may be permitted to put it like that, . . . but John shows his soul."[2]

Each of the Gospels has a different starting point. Matthew begins with Abraham, Mark with John the Baptist, and Luke with Zechariah and Elizabeth. But John's Gospel begins at the beginning—in eternity.

The opening verses are usually described as the Prologue. Like the overture to a great symphony, it introduces the motifs the composer (John) will weave into his testimony to his Lord. What are these motifs?

### The Identity of Jesus

He is the Word made flesh (1:14). With a thrilling use of suspense—read the Prologue slowly and out loud to feel it—John delays before naming the majestic Logos in 1:17–18. Finally, we learn that He is Jesus! He comes to us from the deep recesses of eternity.

Our Savior is the God-man, and we should think of Him as both. In the first verse, He is described as the companion of God (He "was with God") who, simultaneously, is Himself God ("the Word was God"). He "became flesh" (1:14). Fully God, fully man; truly God, truly man.

This view of Jesus—what came to be known in Christian theology as the hypostatic, or "personal," union (our Lord has two natures united in one person)—is the basic key to John's Gospel. The One who strides through its pages is God the Son made flesh.

## Revelation in Jesus

Our Lord is the Light of the World (John 1:4–5, 9; cf. 8:12). John's Gospel records Jesus' self-revelation. Its two main sections are sometimes called the "Book of Signs" (chapters 1–12), in which He points to His own identity, and the "Book of Glory" (chapters 13–21), in which He reveals His fellowship with the Father and the Spirit, and then is glorified through His death, resurrection, and ascension. Throughout both sections, the Lord is light shining into the world's darkness.

In the Book of Signs, Jesus is seen to illumine and expose the darkness that forms the atmosphere in which humanity lives. Thus, Nicodemus, despite his many good qualities, comes to Jesus "by night" (John 3:2). Jesus' conversation with him makes clear that, scholar though he may be, he is spiritually in the dark.

In the Book of Glory, Christ's light continues to shine despite the efforts of the powers of darkness to extinguish it. Again, significantly, when Judas leaves the gathering in the upper room to betray Jesus, "it was night" (13:30).

Into this world in which "men loved darkness rather than light" (3:19), the Light of the World comes to unmask and to judge sin (9:39), and to reveal God. Whoever has seen Him has seen the Father (14:9; cf. 1:18).

## Fulfillment in Jesus

John's Christology is set within the context of God's progressive purposes in history. "The law was given through Moses, but grace and truth came through Jesus Christ" (1:17). The Old Testament points forward to the New. God revealed Himself in pictures and ceremonies through Moses; Jesus is the reality to which they pointed. In Him, fullness arrives (1:16).

Like John the Baptist (1:15), the Law and the Prophets were only witnesses to the Light; Jesus is the Light itself. That is why, for John, the events, imagery, and language of the Old Testament are like a shadow cast backward into history by Christ, the Light of the World. The dwelling of God in the wilderness tabernacle foreshadowed the presence of the Word incarnate as the final temple. It is in Him alone that we finally see God's glory (1:14).

## The Work of Jesus

The Creator is also Re-Creator. From the beginning of his book, John makes clear his answer to the famous question that formed the title of Anselm of Canterbury's great work: *Cur Deus Homo?*—Why the God-man?

What makes this two-nature Christology essential to the gospel? John's answer is twofold:

1. Only God—the One through whom "all things were made" (1:3, cf. v. 10), in whom "was life" and "light" (v. 4)—can reverse creation's death and dissipate the darkness caused by sin.

2. But since that death and darkness are within creation, within man, the Word must become flesh in order to restore it from within. The Creator must enter His own creation, groaning as it is under the burden of alienation from Him.

John's Christology is a Christology from above and from below. Christ comes from the Father, but He is also born of the Virgin Mary. But it is more than that. It is a Christology from without and from within: "How great is the difference between the spiritual glory of the Word of God and the stinking filth of our flesh!" writes Calvin again. "Yet the Son of God stooped so low as to take to himself that flesh addicted to so many wretchednesses."[3]

Thus, John bids us take three steps to understand the Lord Jesus Christ:

1. The Word became flesh.
2. The Word made His dwelling among us.
3. The Word revealed His glory.

When we come to know Christ as our Redeemer, we discover—to our amazement and joy—that we also have come to know our Creator! Then we say, "We have seen His glory."

The lesson? Read and re-read John's Gospel until you discover that it is bigger on the inside than it appeared to be from the outside. That is true of the Gospel of John because it is first true of the gospel of Jesus Christ!

# 2

# SANTA CHRIST?

I took the hand of my toddler son (it was several decades ago now) as we made our way into the local shop on the small and remote Scottish island where earlier that year I had been installed as minister. It was Christmas week. The store was brightly decorated and a general air of excitement was abroad.

Without warning, the conversations of the customers were brought to a halt by a questioning voice from beside me. My son's upraised index finger pointed at a large cardboard Santa Claus. "Daddy, *who* is that *funny-looking* man?" he asked.

Amazement spread across the faces of the jostling shoppers; accusing glances were directed at me. Such shame—the minister's son did not even recognize Santa Claus! What likelihood, then, of hearing good news in his preaching at the festive season?

Such experiences can make us bewail how the Western world gives itself over annually to its Claus-mass or commerce-mass. We celebrate a reworked pagan Saturnalia of epic proportions, one in which the only connection with the incarnation is semantic. Santa is worshiped, not the Savior; pilgrims go to the stores with credit cards, not to the manger with gifts. It is the feast of indulgence, not of the incarnation.

It is always easier to lament and critique the new paganism of secularism's blatant idolatry than to see how easily the church—and we ourselves—twist or dilute the message of the incarnation in order to suit our own tastes. But, sadly, we have various ways of turning the Savior into a kind of Santa Claus.

## *Santa Claus Christianity*

For one thing, in our worship at Christmas we may varnish the staggering truth of the incarnation with what is visually, audibly, and aesthetically pleasing. We confuse emotional pleasure—or worse, sentiment—with true adoration.

For another thing, we may denigrate our Lord with a Santa Claus Christology. How sadly common it is for the church to manufacture a Jesus who is a mirror reflection of Santa Claus. He becomes Santa Christ.

Santa Christ is sometimes a Pelagian Jesus. Like Santa, he simply asks us whether we have been good. More exactly, since the assumption is that we are all naturally good, Santa Christ asks us whether we have been "good enough." So just as Christmas dinner is simply the better dinner we really deserve, Jesus becomes a kind of added bonus who makes a good life even better. He is not seen as the Savior of helpless sinners.

Or Santa Christ may be a Semi-Pelagian Jesus—a slightly more sophisticated Jesus who, Santa-like, gives gifts to those who have already done the best they could! Thus, Jesus' hand, like Santa's sack, opens only when we can give an upper-percentile answer to the none-too-weighty probe, "Have you done your best this year?" The only difference from medieval theology here is that we do not use its Latin phraseology: *facere quod in se est* (to do what one is capable of doing on one's own, or, in common parlance, "Heaven helps those who help themselves").

Then again, Santa Christ may be a mystical Jesus, who, like Santa Claus, is important because of the good experiences we have when we think about him, irrespective of his historical reality. It doesn't really matter whether the story is true or not; the important thing is the spirit of Santa Christ. For that matter, while it would spoil things to tell the children this, everyone can make up his or her own Santa Christ. As long as we have the right spirit of Santa Christ, all is well.

But Jesus is not to be identified with Santa Claus; worldly thinking—however much it employs Jesus-language—is not to be confused with biblical truth.

## *The Christ of Christmas*

The Scriptures systematically strip away the veneer that covers the real truth of the Christmas story. Jesus did not come to add to our comforts. He did not come to help those who were already helping themselves or to fill life with more pleasant experiences. He came on a deliverance mission, to save sinners, and to do so He had to destroy the works of the Devil (Matt. 1:21; 1 John 3:8b).

Those whose lives were bound up with the events of the first Christmas did not find His coming an easy and pleasurable experience.

Mary and Joseph's lives were turned upside down.

The shepherds' night was frighteningly interrupted, and their futures potentially radically changed.

The magi faced all kinds of inconvenience and family separation.

Our Lord Himself, conceived before wedlock, born probably in a cave, would spend His early days as a refugee from the bloodthirsty and vindictive Herod (Matt. 2:13–21).

There is, therefore, an element in the Gospel narratives that stresses that the coming of Jesus is a disturbing event of the deepest proportions. It had to be thus, for He did not come merely to add something extra to life, but to deal with our spiritual insolvency and the debt of our sin. He was not conceived in the womb of Mary for those who have done their best, but for those who know that their best is "like filthy rags" (Isa. 64:6)[4]—far from good enough—and that in their flesh there dwells no good thing (Rom. 7:18). He was not sent to be the source of good experiences, but to suffer the pangs of hell in order to be our Savior.

## *A Christian Christmas*

The Christians who first began to celebrate the birth of the Savior saw this. Christmas for them was not (contrary to what is sometimes mistakenly said) simply adding a Christian veneer to a pagan festival—the Roman Saturnalia. They may have been doing what many Christians have done in marking Reformation Day (which happens to fall on Halloween), namely, committing themselves to a radical alternative to the world's Saturnalia, refusing to be squeezed into its mold. They were determined to fix mind, heart, will, and strength exclusively on the Lord Jesus Christ. There was no confusion in their thinking between the world and the gospel, Saturnalia and Christmas, Santa Jesus and Christ Jesus. They were citizens of another empire altogether.

In fact, such was the malice evoked by their other-worldly devotion to Christ that during the persecutions under the Emperor Diocletian, some believers were murdered as they gathered to celebrate Christmas. What was their gross offense? Worship of the true Christ—incarnate, crucified, risen, glorified, and returning. They celebrated Him that day for giving His all for them, and as they did so, they gave their all for Him.

One Christmas Eve in my teenage years, I opened a book a friend had given to me as a present. I found myself so overwhelmed by its teaching on my recently found Savior that I began to shake with emotion at what had dawned on me: the world had not celebrated His coming, but rather had crucified Him.

Doubtless I was an impressionable teenager. But should it not cause us to tremble that "they crucified my Lord"? Or is that true only in song, not in reality? Are we not there when the world still crucifies Him in its own, often-subtle ways?

The truth is that unless the significance of what Christ did at the first Christmas shakes us, we can scarcely be said to have understood much of what it means, or of who He really is.

*Who is He in yonder stall*
*At Whose feet the shepherds fall?*
*'Tis the Lord! O wondrous story!*
*'Tis the Lord! the King of glory!*
*At His feet we humbly fall,*
*Crown Him! Crown Him, Lord of all!*[5]

And we might add:

*Who is He on yonder cross*
*Suffers for this dark world's loss?*
*'Tis the Lord! O wondrous story!*
*'Tis the Lord! the King of glory!*
*At His feet we humbly fall,*
*Crown Him! Crown Him, Lord of all!*

Let us not confuse Jesus Christ with Santa Claus.

# THE WORD WAS GOD

"Every word that is spoken of himself [Christ]," wrote B. B. Warfield, "is spoken on the assumption that he is God."[6] The first sentence of John's Gospel makes that clear. John believed not only in the Redeemer's pre-existence but also in His absolute deity: "The Word was God" (John 1:1).

Christians have long regarded John's first word about Jesus as the last word on His complete deity. It should not surprise us, therefore, that his testimony has been the object of perennial opposition and attack.

In the early church, such opposition developed into the heresy known as Arianism.[7] Today it is most commonly associated with Jehovah's Witnesses. Their *New World Translation* renders John 1:1 as "the Word was a god." Jesus, they argue, was "divine," but not deity.

Seeing John 1:1 in Greek and in English may help us to follow the argument:

*kai theos ēn ho logos* (Greek text)
and God was the Word (literal English translation)

The Greek word for God is *theos*. Since in the Greek text of John 1:1 the word *theos* lacks the definite article "the" (*ho* in Greek), the *New World Translation* renders it as indefinite ("a god"). Thus, in the view of Jehovah's Witnesses, Jesus is not truly and fully God. At most, He is a divinized creature—"a god."

Why is this translation wrong and the argument that seeks to sustain it an impossible one? There are at least four reasons.

## *Grammar*

In various languages, including Greek, nouns used without the definite article (technically called "anarthrous") are nevertheless frequently definite in meaning.

Later in the first chapter of John, we encounter an interesting example. Nathanael says, "Rabbi, You are the Son of God! You are the King of Israel!" (John 1:49).

In the Greek text, *Son* has the definite article (*ho*), but *King* does not. Yet Nathanael clearly means that Jesus is *the* King, the One God had promised. Thus, even the *New World Translation* renders this verse, "You are King of Israel"—not, notice, *a* king! Jehovah's Witness translators cannot avoid the principle that context determines the translation of an indefinite noun—and should have recognized that in John 1:1.

## *Context*

It is sometimes wittily said that a text without a context becomes a pretext. If the context is the determining factor, what light does it shed on Jesus' identity? John gives us an immediate clue to his meaning: "without Him nothing was made that was made" (John 1:3). The logic of his words requires that our Lord is the Creator and that He Himself is uncreated.

Anyone who has read the Bible from Genesis onward will notice that John attributes to Jesus prerogatives that in the Old Testament belong to God alone. He creates (1:3); He possesses life in Himself (1:4); He "dwelt"—literally "tabernacled"—among men (1:14; the words intentionally remind us of the dwelling of God with His people in the exodus); and He is full of divine glory, grace, and truth (1:14).

## Gospel

John tells us the purpose of his Gospel. He wrote "that you may believe that Jesus is the Christ, the Son of God" (John 20:31). Significantly, this statement immediately follows the dramatic faith-confession of Thomas: "My Lord and my God!" (John 20:28).

Here the Jehovah's Witness translators had no intelligent alternative but to translate the Greek text in the same way as in the *New King James Version*, the *New International Version*, or the *English Standard Version*. The *New World Translation* capitalizes both *Lord* and *God*. Here, in one sentence, Thomas calls Jesus *ho kurios* (the Lord) and *ho theos* (the God). Both words are preceded by the definite article!

Precisely at the climactic point of his Gospel, when he is about to tell us exactly why he wrote his account, John illustrates what happens when faith in Christ is born. He is recognized as truly and fully God.

## Theology

The Prologue to John's Gospel gives us a series of clues to the message of the whole book. In a sense, John is saying, "When you read my Gospel, look for this kind of Savior." And it is precisely His deity that is disclosed. His claims imply equality with the Father, as the Jews recognized (5:17–18). On occasion, He makes that claim explicit (10:30–33).

Our Lord also presents Himself as the One in whom the great I AM of the Old Testament is fully revealed (see Ex. 3:14). For instance, Jesus provides true bread from heaven (John 6:30–51; cf. Deut. 8:16). Likewise, Jesus is the Good Shepherd (Ps. 23; cf. John 10:1ff).

All of this reaches a startling climax at His arrest. Jesus asks the soldiers whom they are seeking. When they tell Him, He replies, "I am He" (18:5).

Jesus' words here clearly echo the covenant divine name *Yahweh*. When He says, "I am He," or "I AM" (*ego eimi*), the soldiers draw back and fall down (18:6).

The event hardly needs a commentary. It is as though, for one brief but amazing moment, Christ's deity cannot remain hidden. Unholy feet cannot remain standing on this holy ground (cf. Ex. 3:5; Ps. 1:5).

## A Reason for John's Words

Why, then, did John not write: "The Word was the God (*ho theos*)?" Because that could have been as misleading as saying, "The Word was a god." It could have suggested that *theos* (God) and *logos* (Word) are mutually exhaustive terms. This, in turn, would have implied that God and Word are mutually exhaustive—with no room for personal distinctions and therefore no room for the Trinity. The Word, or Son, would then simply be a manifestation of God in a temporary form. This idea is what came to be known as Modalism—the heretical view that the Logos is simply one "mode" of God—who sometimes "appears" as Father, sometimes as Son, and sometimes as Spirit, without these being distinct persons.

In saying that the Son is "God with God" (1:1), John is preparing us for a yet fuller revelation: God is Father, Son, and Holy Spirit!

The Gospel of John, indeed the whole Christian faith, stands or falls with John's opening sentence. Christ as deity, God as Trinity, man's salvation—all depend on John's first words.

# 4

# THE HUMANITY
# OF CHRIST

W hy did God become man?" asked Anselm of Canterbury in his famous work with the Latin title, *Cur Deus Homo?* What is the significance of the fact that the Logos became *flesh* (John 1:14)?

No book of the New Testament is more directly concerned with the answer to Anselm's question than the letter to the Hebrews. Although it brings us into the relatively unfamiliar world of Old Testament ritual and theology, a little patient study of its chapters will convince us that here we have one of the profoundest of all biblical revelations of Christ. That is so particularly in what it teaches us about His humanity.

Why did God become man? Among the reasons Hebrews gives us are these:

## Conquest

*The Conquest of Satan required an incarnation.* This is a strange opening note to strike, we might think—until we remember that the Bible's first promise of salvation (in Gen. 3:15) refers not to the forgiveness of Adam's sin but to the overcoming of Adam's enemy, the Devil. Thus, in Hebrews, salvation involves being delivered from Satan's grip. He has "the power of death" and holds men and women in "bondage" by their "fear of death" (2:14–15).

We need *deliverance* as well as pardon.

How can we be delivered? Only if Satan's hold on us is weakened. This can be accomplished only if someone can pay the wages of sin, which gives death its grip and Satan his mastery. To do that requires entering into the experience of death—dying—yet in death overcoming death.

The person who could do this would need to have three qualifications:

1. Be personally free from the need to die for his own sin.
2. Be able and willing to die in order to engage death.
3. Be in possession of the power to recover his life again.

No natural son of Adam could ever meet these qualifications; we have already earned the wages sin inexorably pays in death (Rom. 6:23).

Yet at the same time, no one outside of the human race is capable of possessing these qualifications. This is our plight.

Look then, with joy, at the brilliant divine wisdom in the gospel: "He [Christ] too shared in their humanity so that by his death he might destroy him who holds the power of death—that is, the devil—and free those who all their lives were held in slavery by their fear of death [as the wages of sin]" (Heb. 2:14–15, NIV).

By taking our human nature, Jesus the Son of God lived the life, died the death, and then gained the victory in resurrection that makes freedom from Satan's bondage a reality (see John 8:36).


## *Atonement*

*Atonement was impossible without an incarnation.* Hebrews explains why the Son of God "had to be made like his brothers in every way." It is so "that he might make atonement for the sins of the people" (Heb. 2:17, NIV).

Our salvation requires not only the conquest of our enemy, Satan, but the removal of a yet more terrifying enmity: the wrath of the holy God of heaven. "Purification" and "atonement" must be made "for the sins of the people" (Heb. 1:3; 2:17, NIV).

This was made clear to the people of God in the Old Testament by the constantly repeated ritual sacrifices they were required to make. They thus learned that they deserved death because of their sins; but they also were taught that in grace God Himself provided a sacrifice to take their place.

However, even an Old Testament believer could see that the animal sacrifices could not in themselves make an adequate atonement (Heb. 10:11). Otherwise there would have been no need for them to be repeated. The flesh and blood of bulls and goats could not atone for the sins of human flesh and blood (Heb. 10:4)! Only human flesh and blood could be an appropriate substitute-sacrifice. So the author of Hebrews says:

> When [Christ] came into the world, He said:
> ". . . a body You have prepared for Me.
> In burnt offerings and sacrifices for sin
> You had no pleasure.
> Then I said, 'Behold, I have come—
> In the volume of the book it is written of Me—
> To do your will, O God.'"
>
> —HEBREWS 10:5–7

Jesus offered Himself as the substitutionary atonement!

Sometimes theologians have spoken misleadingly, as though the incarnation is itself the atonement (the "at-one-ment" of God and man in Christ). It is not. But without it there could be no atonement. He took our nature in order to bear our punishment. Only thus can we be at peace with God.

## Comfort

*In our continuing frailty we are comforted by the knowledge of Christ's incarnation.* He entered into our frail human frame, being "made like his brothers in every way" (Heb. 2:17, NIV).

In "every way"—even though He was without sin (Heb. 7:26)? Yes! Remember:

1. His sinlessness did not immunize Him against the *effects* of sin, either during His life or on the cross. In fact, He tasted our temptations with a sen-

sitivity none of us has known precisely because He resisted them. Whatever your experience of temptation or suffering, Christ's was deeper because His humanity was sinless.

2. Only a sinless Savior is able to die for our sins. He cannot die for our sins if He must die for His own. More than that, those who themselves have been overcome by sin cannot ultimately help us to be overcomers. But the incarnate, sinless Son of God can!

Rejoice, then, that "Both the one who makes men holy and those who are made holy are of the same family. So Jesus is not ashamed to call them brothers" (Heb. 2:11, NIV). Rejoice, too, in knowing the "one Mediator between God and men, the Man Christ Jesus" (1 Tim. 2:5)!

# 5

# THE *ARCHĒGOS*

Since the letter to the Hebrews specifically urges Christians to "fix your thoughts on Jesus" (Heb. 3:1, NIV; cf. 12:2), it should not surprise us that the author describes Him in more than a dozen different ways. Jesus is "Son" (1:2); "Lord" (2:3); "Apostle and High Priest" (3:1); "Christ" (5:5); "source of eternal salvation" (5:9, NIV); a priest "according to the order of Melchizedek" (7:11); a descendent of Judah (7:14); "a Minister . . . of the true tabernacle" (8:2); "the Mediator of the new covenant" (9:15; 12:24); "the same yesterday, today, and forever" (13:8); and the "great Shepherd of the sheep" (13:20).

But perhaps the most intriguing title for Jesus in the letter is "author." He is called the "author of . . . salvation" and the "author . . . of our faith" (Heb. 2:10; 12:2, NIV).

This title has a rich connotation. The Greek word translated as "author" is *archēgos*. It expresses the idea of a leader, one who goes at the head of a group to open the way for others.

Think of a troop of commandos operating in a jungle war. They find their way blocked by a deep ravine. The situation is too urgent to find a way around. Their commanding officer manages to throw a rope across and anchor it. He then risks his life by crossing first, hand over hand. He permanently secures the rope. He creates a bridge. The way is now open for his men to cross over to the other side.

This is a pale and inadequate reflection of what the author of Hebrews means by calling Jesus the *archēgos* or "author" of our salvation. Our Lord is the "pioneer" of our salvation; through His suffering, He brings many sons to glory (Heb. 2:10).

## *Archēgos*—First and Second

Adam was the first *archēgos*. He was called to lead the human race in obedience, through testing, to the destination of glory. He sinned and failed, falling short of the glory of God (Rom. 3:23). This world became a jungle where man and God, man and Satan, man and woman, man and beast, man and his environment, and man and his brother have all become entangled in hostility (Gen. 3:8–19; 4:1–12).

Jesus came as the second *archēgos,* the second representative man (1 Cor. 15:45–47). He entered the jungle. He broke through and subdued all its opposition to God. He dealt with God's solemn curse (Gen. 3:14, 17) and opened the way into God's presence for all who believe in and follow Him (Heb. 10:19–20).

The Son of God took our human nature and entered into our fallen, sin-ravaged environment. He lived a life of perfect obedience for the glory of God. Bearing God's judgment against our sin on the cross, He experienced the divine curse. Now divine blessing and restoration flow to us along the path of grace He has opened (Gal. 3:13).

## *Back to the Future*

To be the *archēgos* of such a salvation, the Son of God had to begin at the beginning. In the womb of the Virgin Mary, He took our flesh. He who upholds all things had to become incarnate first as an embryo—small, fragile, dependent on His mother for physical survival. As He did so, the Holy Spirit overshadowed Mary so that although He was the fruit of her womb, He was "the Holy One" (Luke 1:35) from the very moment of His conception.

In Jesus, God began again from the beginning. In a world in which sin infects us all from the womb (Ps. 51:5), it was not possible to begin with a mature man. Our Lord had to begin His work in prenatal darkness, mature through every stage of life in perfect fellowship with His Father, and then die in the deeper darkness that surrounded Him on Golgotha.

Jesus was the only child ever to grow "normally" in "wisdom and stature, and in favor with God and men" (Luke 2:52). It was not, however, in an abundant Eden with perfect parents. It was in a blue-collar home in which even those who loved Him did not always understand Him.

Later, as a mature man of 30, He confronted the tempter, but not in a plentiful garden, supported by a human helper, or accompanied by beasts that would submit to His naming (Gen. 2:15–22). No, Jesus had to claw His way through the desert wilderness that human sin had created. Weakened by hunger and thirst, and surrounded by wild beasts, He had to withstand Satan. Yet there He overcame His enemy, who, serpentlike, crawled from Jesus' holy presence, subdued by His victor's command: "Away with you, Satan!" (Matt. 4:10).

After a life of obedience, the captain of our salvation, although tortured and beaten, by His sacrificial death overcame every obstacle barring the way to fellowship with His Father. He bore our sin; He died to its dominion and thus defeated Satan. By His resurrection He overcame death, opening a "new and living way" to the holy presence of God for all who believe (Heb. 10:20). From womb to cradle, from desert to Golgotha, from tomb to throne, our Lord Jesus blazed a trail of grace. He is our *archēgos*!

And so we can sing with Charles Wesley:

*Soar we now where Christ has led,*
*Following our exalted Head;*
*Made like him, like him we rise;*
*Ours the cross, the grave, the skies.*

*Hail the Lord of earth and heaven!*
*Praise to thee by both be given;*
*Thee we greet triumphant now;*
*Hail, the Resurrection, thou!*[8]

# He Stoops to Conquer

W e are in the upper room. The "Book of Signs" (John 1–12) has been closed; now the "Book of Glory" (John 13–22) is opened. So close is the fellowship of the apostolic band here that the beloved disciple can simply lean back in order to talk to Jesus (John 13:25). Here, if anywhere, we see why Calvin commented that while the Synoptic Gospels show us Christ's body, John shows us His soul. A veil has been drawn between Christ and the world; but to "his own" He now reveals "the full extent of his love" (13:1, NIV).

The foot-washing scene follows (13:1–17). Its inner meaning will not be understood until later (13:7). But it becomes clear to John, as he explains (13:1): Jesus is revealing the heart of both His identity and His ministry. In a remarkable way, the event is an acted parable for which Paul's great exposition in Philippians 2:5–11 provides the theological commentary.

We can see this most clearly if we follow the steps Jesus takes:

## *Origin*

John gives us a poignant insight into the mindset of our Lord. He is profoundly conscious of His place in the divine fellowship: He has come from the Father, has exercised the power of the Father, and is now returning to the Father (John 13:3)—although He has never left His Father's side (1:18; 5:19–20).

In the full consciousness of this dignity, Jesus now shows how much He loves His disciples by leaving His position at the head of the table, taking off His seamless outer garment, and dressing in servant garb to fulfill a servant's task. The Lord of Glory washes dirty feet.

**Commentary on Step One:** "Who, being in the form of God . . . made Himself of no reputation, taking the form of a bondservant" (Phil. 2:6–7).

## Salvation

The Lord of all becomes the servant of all. Echoes of the graphic description of the Suffering Servant of Isaiah 52:13–53:12 can be heard in the upper room. Indeed, the pattern of the passage in John 13:1–17 is one and the same as Philippians 2:5–11: humbling is the way to glorification.

But our Lord's self-humbling is not merely exemplary (although it is that, too, vv. 14–15); it is saving. Jesus does not stoop merely in order to shame the disciples, but to show them that the only way of salvation is through His washing away the filth of their sins by His self-emptying on the cross. Only those who are washed can have any part in Jesus (13:8).

**Commentary on Step Two:** "Being found in appearance as a man, He humbled Himself and became obedient to the point of death, even the death of the cross" (Phil. 2:8).

## Exaltation

When Jesus finished washing the disciples' feet, "He put on his clothes and returned to his place" (John 13:12, NIV). The language here echoes Jesus' earlier words: "The reason my Father loves me is that I lay down my life— only to take it up again. . . . I have authority to lay it down and authority to take it up again" (10:17–18, NIV).

Once again, our Lord illustrates in the microcosm of the upper room what was prophesied of the Suffering Servant: from exaltation, He stoops in humiliation. But His humiliation leads to exaltation (Isa. 52:13; 53:11–12).

**Commentary on Step Three:** "Therefore God also has highly exalted Him and given Him the name which is above every name, that at the name of Jesus every knee should bow . . ." (Phil. 2:9–10).

## Application

The acted parable of the upper room concludes with Jesus asking the disciples: "Do you know what I have done to you?" (John 13:12). He encourages them to reflect on what they have just seen. Have they understood the implications of being the disciples of such a Teacher and the servants of such a Lord (13:13)?

Jesus catechizes them, albeit informally, because He wants to make sure that the inner logic of the occasion will transform the way they think and live (Rom. 12:1–2). Do they understand the power of Jesus' words, "If I . . . therefore you"? Those who receive the cleansing that comes freely to them, yet at such cost to Him, must be "Christians with attitude"—the attitude that comes from fellowship with Christ (Phil. 2:5). As the Master lives, so must the servant.

Our Lord's catechizing bears fruit. It is not only on John that this event leaves an indelible impression. Twice Simon Peter echoes its language. First in a general way: "Christ also suffered for us, leaving us an example, that you should follow His steps" (1 Peter 2:21). Then, even more poignantly: "All of you be submissive to one another, and be clothed with humility" (1 Peter 5:5). It is surely not accidental that he uses what J. N. D. Kelly calls "working-class"[9] language here—language appropriate to those who are prepared to wear the servant's livery as bond-slaves of Christ and who are willing to be the bond-slaves of others (2 Cor. 4:5).

Did Peter remember how slow he was—in the upper room, as well as before and after—to appreciate what it really meant for Jesus to be his Savior?

**Commentary on Step Four:** "Do nothing out of selfish ambition or vain conceit, but in humility consider others better than yourselves. Each of you should look not only to his own interests, but also to the interests of others. Your attitude should be the same as that of Christ Jesus" (Phil. 2:3–5, NIV).

Is your attitude "the same as that of Christ Jesus"?

# PART II

---

# The Heart
# of the Matter

*Jesus is our Savior. But those simple words summarize glorious and deep truths about what He has done for us. This is why Paul speaks about "the surpassing worth of knowing Christ Jesus my Lord" (Phil. 3:8, ESV).*

# THE ROMANS EXCHANGE

When the wonder of the gospel breaks into your life, you feel as though you are the first person to discover its power and glory. Where has Christ been hidden all these years? He seems so fresh, so new, so full of grace. Then comes a second discovery—it is you who have been blind, but now you have experienced exactly the same as countless others before you. You compare notes. Sure enough, you are not the first! Thankfully you will not be the last.

## *Discovering a Key*

If my own experience is anything by which to judge, discovering Romans can be a similar experience.

I still remember, as a Christian teenager, the slow dawning of this thought in my mind: all Scripture is God-breathed and useful to me, but it also seems to have a shape and structure, a center and circumference. If that is so, then some biblical books may be foundational; these should be mastered first.

Then came the realization that (alongside systematic theologies) biblical commentaries must be the foundation of my book collection. Blessed in the Scotland of those days with free tuition and a student allowance, I purchased the wonderful studies of Romans by Robert Haldane and John Murray. (Only later did it strike me that a certain ethnic prejudice may have been present in me, since both were Scots!)

As I studied Romans, wrestling with some of its great truths, struggling with some of its tough passages (surely it is to them that 2 Peter 3:14–16 refers!), it became clear that countless feet had walked this way before. I had only just begun to join them in discovering the mind-renewing, life-changing power of what Paul calls "the gospel of God" (Rom. 1:1; 15:16), "the gospel of Christ" (Rom. 1:16; 15:19), and "my gospel" (Rom. 2:16; 16:25). Soon it became clear why Martin Luther called Romans "the clearest gospel of all."[10]

## The Great Exchange

The gospel of Romans can be summarized in one word: *exchange*. In fact, as Paul summarizes the teaching of Romans 1:18–5:11, he concludes that Christians "rejoice in God through our Lord Jesus Christ, through whom we have now received the *reconciliation*" (Rom. 5:11, emphasis added). The root meaning of the Greek word *katallagē,* translated "reconciliation," is a change (or exchange) taking place.[11]

Paul's gospel is the story of a series of exchanges.

**Exchange number one** is described in 1:18–32: knowing the clearly revealed Creator God who has displayed His glory in the universe He has made, humanity has "*[ex]changed* the glory of the incorruptible God into an image . . . *exchanged* the truth of God for the lie, and worshiped and served the creature rather than the Creator . . . *exchanged* the natural use for what is against nature" (1:23–26, emphasis added)—all variations on the same root.

**Exchange number two** is the direct, divinely ordained consequence of this: God exchanged the privilege of man's communion-knowledge of Him for His righteous wrath against man (Rom. 1:18ff). Instead of knowing, trusting, and lovingly glorifying God, mankind by its ungodliness and unrighteousness (the order is significant) drew forth God's judgment.

Thus, communion with God was exchanged for condemnation by God. Neither is this merely eschatological, far off in the future; it is invasive in a contemporary way. Men and women give God up and flaunt their pretended autonomy in His face. They think, "We despise His laws and break them freely, yet no threatened thunderbolt of judgment touches us." In fact, however, they are judicially blinded and hardened. They cannot see that the conscience-hardening and body-destroying effects of their rebellion *are* the judgment of God. His judgments are righteous—if we will have ungodliness, then the punishment will come through the very instruments of our crime against Him. In the end, we have exchanged the light of His presence for present inner darkness and future outer darkness.

**Exchange number three** is the gracious, unmerited (in fact, *demerited*) exchange that God provided in Christ. Without compromise of His righteousness revealed in wrath, God righteously justifies sinners through the redemption He provided in Christ's blood-propitiation for our sins. This Paul states in the rich and tightly-packed words of Romans 3:21–26.

It is only later in the letter that he gives us a different, and in some ways more fundamental, way of looking at this: the Son of God took our nature and came "in the likeness of sinful flesh" (Rom. 8:3) in order to exchange places with Adam, so that His obedience and righteousness might for our sakes be exchanged for Adam's (and our) disobedience and sin (Rom. 5:12–21).

**Exchange number four** is that which is offered to sinners in the gospel: righteousness and justification instead of unrighteousness and condemnation. Moreover, this Christ-shaped righteousness was constituted by His entire life of obedience and His wrath-embracing sacrifice on the cross, where He was made a sin offering (He came, says Paul in Rom. 8:3, "on account of sin," or "to be a sin offering"; NIV).

In addition to insisting on the fact that this divine exchange is consistent with the absolute righteousness of God (Rom. 3:21, 22, 25, 26), Paul stresses that this way of salvation is consistent with the teaching of the Old Testament ("being witnessed by the Law and the Prophets," v. 21; cf. 1:1–4). He also insists that we contribute nothing to our salvation. It is all of grace. The sheer genius of the divine strategy is simply breathtaking.

**Exchange number five** emerges here.

In the *Institutes of the Christian Religion*, when John Calvin moves from Book II (on the work of Christ) to Book III (on the application of redemption), he writes:

We must now examine this question. How do we receive those benefits which the Father bestowed on his only-begotten Son—not for Christ's own private use, but that he might enrich poor and needy men? First, we must understand that as long as Christ remains outside of us, and we are separated from him, all that he has suffered and done for the salvation of the human race remains useless and of no value to us . . . we obtain this *by faith*.[12]

In response to the great exchange that has been accomplished *for us* in Christ, there is an exchange accomplished *in us* by the Spirit: unbelief gives way to faith, rebellion is exchanged for trust. Justification—our being declared righteous and constituted in a righteous relationship with God—is not made ours by works, ceremonial or otherwise, but by the exercise of faith in Christ.

## By Faith

Paul expresses himself at this point with great care and states the relationship between faith and justification with meticulous precision. Justification is always said to be "by faith," never "on account of/on the basis of faith (*dia pistin*)." Faith is not the ground or basis upon which we are justified, but the means, the "instrument," by which we are united to Christ, in whom our justification, our "right-wising" with God, has been accomplished. In Archbishop William Temple's words, "All is of God; the only thing of my very own which I contribute to my redemption is the sin from which I need to be redeemed."[13]

This is clear enough in what Paul says in his basic exposition. It is made even clearer in his application of that exposition in Romans 3:27–30. Here he argues that all boasting in relationship to justification is excluded. But then he probes the question: why? He asks, "By what law [i.e., principle]? Of works? No, but by the law of faith."

In one sense, of course, boasting is excluded by the law of works, since we cannot perfectly perform them, and even if we could, either personal or ceremonial works would be inadequate to deal with our guilt and sin. But that does not seem to be Paul's point. Rather, it is that faith as the way of receiving justification excludes the possibility of boasting. Faith, by definition, excludes all contribution on our part.

But how can this be, when faith is an activity in which we consciously engage? It is not God who believes for us; it is we who believe.

The genius of the divine way of salvation by faith is that in it we are personally, actively united to Jesus Christ, but in a way that contributes nothing to His work. Faith is by definition noncontributory; it is the reception of Christ, not an addition to His finished work.

B. B. Warfield finely puts it this way:

It is not faith that saves, but faith in Jesus Christ. . . . It is not, strictly speaking, even faith in Christ that saves, but Christ that saves through faith. The saving power resides exclusively, not in the act of faith or the attitude of faith or in the nature of faith, but in the object of faith.[14]

In this sense, even though we are actively involved in faith, we are passive with respect to the accomplishing of justification. In the deepest sense, then, it is by grace that we are saved through faith, and that (whether the grace, the faith, or the union of the two in justification) is the gift of God; it is not of works, lest anyone should boast (Eph. 2:8–9; notice the reiteration of the theme of non-boasting of Rom. 3:27).

In the light of this, when Paul later says that faith *was accounted* to Abraham for righteousness" (Rom. 4:9, emphasis added), he is obviously not contradicting himself. He is simply citing Genesis 15:6 and seeing that statement as a shorthand summary of his own teaching that we are justified because we believe in God's promise of salvation accomplished in Christ and received by faith.

This gospel of God, Paul's gospel, is massive. And what makes it so is grace—sheer, undiluted, overwhelming grace. Massive indeed! That is why the same Luther who called Romans "the clearest gospel of all" recognized the appropriateness to Romans not only of Jeremiah 9:23–24 ("Let him who boasts boast in [the Lord]"; ESV) but also of earlier words of Jeremiah:

The sum and substance of this letter is to pull down, pluck up and destroy all wisdom and righteousness of the flesh . . . no matter how heartily and sincerely they may be practiced. . . . As Christ says through the prophet Jeremiah, "to pluck up and to break down and to destroy and to overthrow" (Jer. 1:10), namely everything that is in us (i.e., all that pleases us because it comes from ourselves and belongs to us) and "to build and to plant," namely everything that is outside of us and in Christ.[15]

To engage in the lifelong task of studying, being mastered by, and mastering Romans is to discover the aptness of Luther's allusion. For this gospel of grace involves us in the ongoing discovery that there is still much in our lives that has not yielded to the demolition power of grace; and much remains yet to be built by grace. That is why Romans is the clearest *gospel* of all!

# HEBREWS—DOES IT
# DO ANYTHING FOR YOU?

A friend—his face wrinkled in a cheerful grin—described a conversation he had overheard at the end of a conference address I had given. One hearer, apparently full of the blessings of the passage that had been considered, turned to his neighbor—a stranger to him—and made some positive comments on the experience of the preceding hour: "Wasn't that great?" He received a somewhat chilling reply: "Didn't do anything for me!"

I suspect that if one were to do a kind of New Testament Random Letter Association Test (to be known among evangelicals in the future as the NTRLA Test!), Philippians ("full of joy"), Romans ("full of the doctrines of grace"), and even James ("full of practical counsel") would fare well. But the mention of Hebrews might evoke a substantial number of "Does nothing for me" responses.

Is it too different, too alien in thought, too "Old Testamentish"? Whatever the reason, Hebrews rarely stands high on the list of beloved parts of the New Testament—apart, of course, from the occasional memorized verse about temptation, faith, or looking to Jesus.

Yet there is no letter in the New Testament that tells us more about Christ and His work; chapter after chapter unfolds—ten in all—before we come to the hinge that brings the unknown author from exposition of Christ ("holy brethren . . . consider the Apostle and High Priest of our confession, Christ Jesus," Heb. 3:1) to application ("Therefore, . . . let us . . . ," Heb. 10:19, 22).

So few things would do the evangelical church more good than a baptism into the letter to the Hebrews! But why? Here are several reasons, selected almost randomly from a cursory reading of the letter:

## Christ, the Key to the Old Testament

*Hebrews reveals Christ as the key to understanding the Old Testament.* Gentle reader, that is 75 percent of your Bible! Hebrews acts as a master interpreter, taking you through the pages of the Old Testament and highlighting its central message. It provides a sure-footed guide to the way in which various elements in the Old Testament combine to lead to Jesus—history, liturgy, typology, and prophecy are all woven together into a harmonious portrayal of the significance of His ministry. The whole book unfolds the statement with which it opens:

> *God, who at various times and in various ways spoke in time past to the fathers by prophets, has in these last days spoken to us by His Son, whom He has appointed heir of all things, through whom also He made the worlds.*
>
> —HEBREWS 1:1–2

| The Old Testament message is: | The New Testament message is: |
| --- | --- |
| *In time past* | *Now, in the last days* |
| *multifaceted revelation* | *focused revelation* |
| *expressed through the prophets* | *expressed in Christ the Son* |
| *given to the fathers* | *given to us* |

The two are related—as Hebrews explains—as promise and fulfillment; type and antitype; shadow and reality. They are bound together by one promise, one plan of salvation, one way of grace, one Savior. Therefore, understand Hebrews and you will be able to read the Old Testament with spectacles that will help you to see how it all makes unified, glorious, Christ-centered sense!

## Christ Jesus—the Great One

*Hebrews displays the greatness of Jesus Christ.* The New Testament never despises the Old. But sometimes its language seems to verge on the pejorative. The reason for this is simple. In the light of the full, magnificent revelation of God's grace in Christ, everything that preceded it fades by comparison.

So Hebrews is at pains to point out the superiority of Christ over angels, Moses, Joshua, Aaron and the priesthood, the tabernacle, and sacrifices—in fact, over everything and everyone revered for a role in the giving and effecting of the "old" Mosaic covenant. Now that the new has come, the old begins to look poor, preliminary, and even tawdry *by comparison.*

This, of course, harmonizes with Pauline teaching. Our Lord Jesus is simply "the Greatest!"

## The Humanity of Jesus

*Hebrews emphasizes the theological and practical importance of the humanity of Christ.* This emerges again and again in the letter.

Underline this thought: assurance, peace, access to God, knowledge that He is our Father, and strength to overcome temptation all depend on this— the Son of God took our flesh and bore our sins in such a way that further sacrifice for sin is both unnecessary and unintelligible. Christ died our death, and now in His resurrection He continues to wear our nature forever, and in it He lives for us before the face of God. He could not do more for us than He has done; we need no other resources to enable us to walk through this world into the next.

You and I need a Savior who is near us, is one with us, understands us. All of this the Lord Jesus is, Hebrews affirms. Fix your gaze on this Christ and your whole Christian life will be transformed.

## *The Nature of True Faith*

*Hebrews emphasizes the nature of true faith in the Lord Jesus Christ.* The unnamed first recipients of this letter were under pressure to return to their old ways and their old religion. The author, however, was convinced that despite the temptations, despite their failures, salvation was theirs because they had the kind of faith that would persevere to the end (Heb. 6:11).

In this they were one with the great heroes of faith in the past, from Abel onward, all of whom, according to the extent of God's revelation given to them, looked forward to the fulfillment of all His promises in Christ. All of them counted suffering disgrace (and all of them did suffer it) for the sake of the (promised) Christ of greater value than all the treasures of this world.

If studying Hebrews had that effect on us, it would be time well spent, don't you think?

How do you feel about Hebrews "doing" that for you?

# 9

# CHRIST OF THE THREE APPEARINGS

Many pastors, perhaps most, take a very deep breath before they commit themselves to preaching through the letter to the Hebrews! This is understandable, for the book brings most Christians into a world that is alien and distant: Melchizedek and Aaron, temple and furniture, blood and animal sacrifices, types and antitypes. This is a strange old world indeed!

Yet Hebrews is a key to the entire Bible, a road map to the whole history of redemption, as its opening verses make clear. And from time to time—as in those lofty opening verses—the author provides us with remarkable, and in some senses "simple," summaries of the saving plan of God. In addition, he occasionally provides outlines that help us to see our own lives in the context of God's ongoing purposes.

One such summary comes in Hebrews 9:24–28. Within a few sentences, the author uses the verb *appear* three times with reference to three distinct events in the ministry of the Lord Jesus. He mentions them in the order of the argument he is pursuing; their significance underlines the way in which he thinks of Christ's work.

First, Christ has appeared once for all to put away sin by His sacrifice (Heb. 9:26b).

Second, Christ now appears in the presence of God on our behalf (Heb. 9:24).

Third, Christ will appear to save those who are waiting eagerly for Him (Heb. 9:28).

## Three Tenses

The dimensions of Christ's work are expressed in three tenses. He has appeared (past), He now appears (present), and He will appear (future). This helps us to appreciate and understand the wonder of God's plan in history by illumining the experience of old and new covenant believers and by teaching us the dimensions of Christ's High Priestly ministry on our behalf.

In this way we learn to think like the biblical scholar, who, when asked by an enthusiastic believer whether he was saved, gave this answer (alluding to the past, present, and future tenses in which the verb *save* is used in the New Testament): "Do you mean have I been saved, am I being saved, or will I be saved?" All three are true; all three help us better appreciate our Lord's work.

So when believers ask us (as some do a great deal!): "Do you believe in the 'appearing' of the Lord?" we might similarly respond, "Do you mean His first appearing, His present appearing, or His future appearing?" We believe in, and are saved by, all three. They all are part of His ministry as our High Priest and Savior.

## Past

Christ appeared on earth to put away sin. Unlike the repeated sacrifices offered by the Aaronic priests, His was a once-for-all sacrifice. That is why the author says He appeared "at the end of the ages" (Heb. 9:26). The work of Christ brings the days of preparation and expectation to an end. His death, resurrection, ascension, and giving of His Spirit usher in "the last days" (Heb.1:2; Acts 2:17).

This perspective helps us to understand spiritual experience in the Old Testament through the eyes of the author. Old covenant believers lived in the light of the promises of God and walked by faith while trying to understand the inner significance of the sacrifices God had provided. They looked at the sacrificial system in order to puzzle over the real, final sacrifice that was being typified. They did not receive what God had promised (Heb. 11:39). Yet they understood that the pattern of repeated sacrifices of animals, by a long line of priests who needed to atone for their own sins, could not be the way of full and final forgiveness (Heb. 9:1–10).

## Present

How privileged we are to live in the age when Christ has appeared and has dealt fully and finally with our sin. But what is Christ doing now? He is appearing in heaven to intercede for His people (Heb. 9:24). Here the author of Hebrews is thinking of what took place after the death of our High Priest.

When our Christ went before God at Calvary, He carried no other sacrifice than Himself. There, in the true Holy of Holies, in the darkness of Golgotha, He was "stricken, smitten by God, and afflicted" (Isa. 53:4). Suddenly He cried, "My God, My God, why have You forsaken Me?" His body, dead under the weight of our sins, was thereafter laid in the garden tomb.

When the high priest made his sacrifices, bells on the hem of his garment sounded so that the worshipers from whom he was hidden would know he was still alive (Ex. 28:33–35). By contrast, no bells sounded during the long hours in which Christ lay buried in the garden tomb. But then He came forth; He rose in the power of an indestructible life and ascended to the right hand of the Father. There He appears for us—evidence (if ever it was needed) that His sacrifice for our sins has been accepted and that it never needs to be repeated.

Now Christ embodies in Himself the propitiation He made for our sins (Rev. 5:6). Jesus' appearance at God's right hand is the intercession we need (Rom. 8:34; 1 John 2:1–2)!

## Future

So long as Jesus Christ is there, in heaven before God for us, our salvation will last. We know He is there forever (Heb. 7:25). But something else lies in the future. Christ will appear in glory to save those who eagerly await Him (Heb. 9:28).

We often say Christians live "between the times," tasting the "already" or "now" of salvation but conscious that there is a "not yet" about our experience. The author of Hebrews understood that the same pattern was true of Old Testament believers. They lived believing the promise of Christ but before His coming.

Now the author underlines how—in the light of the first two appearances of Christ—there remains a "not yet" for us as new covenant believers. We are not yet home with Christ; the pilgrimage continues until He appears for the last time fully and finally to save us.

Note well the description of those Christ will save. They are "those who eagerly wait for Him" (Heb. 9:28). A glorious paradox indeed: waiting—but eagerly (cf. Rom. 8:25)! Does this description fit you?

The three appearances of Christ help us understand the gospel. But they also cause us to search our hearts. The first two appearances of the Lord Jesus are meant to give us such an appreciation for what Christ has done and is doing that we eagerly wait for Him.

How eager are you?

# 10

# REAL PRIEST,
# EFFECTIVE SACRIFICE

The High Priesthood of Jesus Christ is a recurring theme in Hebrews. Several aspects of this ministry are stressed:

*Christ is a true High Priest.* He is properly qualified to represent us because He became one with us in the weakness and frailty of our flesh, experiencing suffering and the inevitable exposure to our temptations (Heb. 2:14–18).

*Jesus is the Great High Priest.* In Him the symbolism of the Day of Atonement is fulfilled. He personally *offered* the sacrifice for the sins of the people (Lev. 16:9); but more than that, He *was* the sacrifice. Christ offered not merely the blood of animals but His own precious blood (Heb. 9:14, 25).

*Jesus is a superior High Priest.* He completed the purification for sins— something the Old Testament priests could never do. They needed to stand *daily* at the Jerusalem altar, repeating the same sacrifices. But Christ's sufficient sacrifice was made once for all. We know this because, after He made it, He "*sat down* at the right hand of the Majesty on high" (Heb. 1:3, emphasis added; cf. 10:11–12).

Furthermore, the Levitical priests died. Their ministry was brief and passing. But Christ's priesthood is eternal, exercised in "the power of an endless life" (Heb. 7:11–16). He is a High Priest forever, able to save us completely (Heb. 7:23–25).

## *Reality Behind the Copy*

It is common to think of the Old Testament ritual as providing the model that Jesus' priesthood subsequently copied and fulfilled. But Hebrews sees things differently. The Old Testament ritual of the high priest moving through the tabernacle—with its various rooms and furniture, especially the Holy of Holies and the ark with the mercy seat—is not the model but the copy (Heb. 8:5).

Christ has made a way into heaven; that is the reality. Hebrews has much to say about this. Jesus "went through the greater and more perfect tabernacle that is . . . not a part of this creation" (Heb. 9:11, NIV). "With His own blood He entered the Most Holy Place once for all" (Heb. 9:12). In fact, Jesus now ministers in the heavenly tabernacle (Heb. 8:2).

## *Copy of the True*

Notice what grips the mind of the author: if the copy (the wilderness tabernacle) needed purification, then the "heavenly things themselves [had to be purified] with better sacrifices" (Heb. 9:23). But what is this purifying of heavenly things?

For the people to be brought symbolically and temporarily into the presence of God, every part of the tabernacle had to be ritually cleansed, since nothing defiled could be employed in man's approach to a holy God (Heb. 9:19–23). Therefore, on the Day of Atonement, Aaron slew a sacrifice, entered the Holy of Holies with the blood, and poured it out on the mercy seat between the cherubim (Lev. 16:15–16).

This ritual was an acted parable, a copy of what Christ was to do on the great day when He made atonement. The blood of animals is both inappropriate and inadequate to provide the cleansing necessary to approach God. Animal sacrifice could not atone for human sin. Neither could any finite individual atone for sin against the infinite God. Only the blood of the divine image incarnate could cleanse our sin and enable us to enter safely into the presence of God, who is a consuming fire (Heb. 1:3; 12:29).

The work of atonement took place in the presence of the God of heaven. Indeed, it involved a transaction within the fellowship of the persons of the eternal Trinity in their love for us: the Son was willing, with the aid of the Spirit, to experience the hiding of the Father's face. The shedding of the blood of God's Son opened the way to God for us (Acts 20:28). That is both the horror and the glory of our Great High Priest's ministry.

## Terrible Means, Glorious End

This is theology of the most exalted and mind-stunning nature. It dwarfs our sometimes overly pragmatic view of what is central to real spirituality. Yet what makes such theology so awe-inspiring is this—God is here at His most pragmatic; a glorious end justifies the most terrible means. Without those means there can be no remission of sins. Here theology of the deepest kind is pragmatism of the highest order.

Take time to meditate long and hard on this aspect of Christ's priesthood and on its implications. Hebrews refers to at least four conclusions to be drawn. Since you have such a Great High Priest, who by His blood has opened a new and living way into the Most Holy Place (10:19–20):

- Draw near to God in full assurance (10:22).
- Do not draw back from running the Christian race (10:39).
- Fix your eyes on Jesus since He is such a great Savior (12:1–2).
- Be prepared to go outside the camp, sharing Christ's humiliation (13:13–14).

This is the pathway on which Christ will lead you into the presence of God.

# 11

# High Priest
# and Intercessor

ebrews is the only book in the New Testament that describes Jesus as our High Priest. But the idea lingers in the background of the entire New Testament. For instance, Paul tells us that Christ intercedes for us (Rom. 8:34) and John tells us that Christ is our advocate with the Father (1 John 2:1).

Throughout the centuries, Christians have read John 17 against this background. Reading it, Cyril of Alexandria (d. 444) described Jesus as a high priest making intercession for his people. And the Lutheran theologian David Chytraus (1531–1600) called the chapter our Lord's "High Priestly Prayer."

This passage provides a wonderful insight into the heart of Christ and His concern for His people.

### Qualifications for High Priests

In the ritual theology of the Old Testament, several important things prepared an individual to be a high priest.

First, the priest had to feel for and share the weaknesses of his people (Heb. 5:2). In John 13:21, Jesus clearly does this. He is troubled in spirit (cf. John 12:27).

Second, the priest was consecrated to the service of God. Likewise, Jesus sanctifies Himself to the service of God (John 17:19).

Third, the high priest carried the names and needs of God's people. Over his priestly garments, on his shoulders and breastplate, he wore precious stones on which were inscribed the names of the tribes of Israel. Likewise, Jesus carries the burdens and needs of His people to God as He prays for His disciples (John 17:6–19) and all who will become His disciples in the future (John 17:20–26).

## High Priestly Prayer

The Day of Atonement, when the high priest entered into the Holy of Holies to intercede for the people, was the most solemn point of the whole year for Old Testament believers. What would he pray? Would his intercession be accepted? Would he emerge again alive—would the people hear the gentle sound of the bells on his garments again? Every Jew surely would have given anything to have been able to overhear the voice of the high priestly intercessor. But no one ever did.

By contrast, Christians know the subject of the true High Priest's prayer—their vision of His glory: "Father, I desire that they also whom You gave Me may be with Me where I am, that they may behold My glory which You have given Me; for You loved Me before the foundation of the world" (John 17:24). Jesus has already promised them His peace (14:27; 16:33) and His joy (15:11; 16:22). Now He completes the picture: He asks the Father that they may see His glory.

## Glory Instead of Shame

Notice the stark contrast between this petition and the one Jesus offers in Gethsemane. There He is crushed under the dark vision of the cup He is to drink; here He prays in the light of His finished work (17:4). There He prays in the shadow of His impending experience of God-forsakenness; here He prays in the light of the Father's eternal love for Him (17:24).

What we are privileged to overhear, then, is an echo of the eternal fellowship between the Father and the Son. The Father loves the Son and shares His eternal glory with Him.

Glory is virtually the physical manifestation of all the perfections of God's being—His goodness, truth, faithfulness, righteousness, holiness, and wisdom. The Father and Son lived in perfect enjoyment of that glory, in unending mutual love "before the foundation of the world" (17:24). Now, our eternal, divine Lord, who ever dwells by the side of the Father (John 1:18), wants more than anything else in the world that we should see Him in this effulgent glory.

Why?

First, Jesus thinks of us as a love-gift from His Father (17:24). At this sacred moment, Jesus uses the description of His disciples that means most to Him. Christians are they "whom You gave Me." He has nothing He counts more precious. Therefore, He wants us to be with Him forever.

Second, Jesus knows the grief the disciples will feel during His agony in Gethsemane and the humiliation of the cross. Likewise, He knows the pain we feel when people trample His blood underfoot and seek to crucify Him again, subjecting Him to public disgrace (Heb. 10:29; 6:6). So He wants us to see Him as He really is: the Lord enthroned in glory.

Third, Jesus wants us to know that His prayers for our salvation will be heard and answered. Because He asks only for what His Father has promised to give Him, He knows that His Father will not refuse Him.

## Glimpse of Treasures

Can you take in what you have overheard in the High Priestly Prayer of John 17? It is like a light momentarily switched on in a darkened room and then extinguished. Did you really see such treasures? Has Jesus actually prayed that my faith will not fail (Luke 22:31–32) and that I will be kept by God's power for such glory (1 Peter 1:5–11)? Is even my name engraved on His shoulders and inscribed on His heart?

Do you understand how much your High Priest cares for you and loves you? It is almost as though He were saying, "Father, My glory will be incomplete unless You keep this promise—that My beloved disciples can see it and share it."

Think of it: "Jesus Christ is the same yesterday, today, and forever" (Heb. 13:8).

# 12

# CHRIST THE KING

W here is He who has been born King of the Jews?" asked the unexpected visitors from the East who appeared on Herod's doorstep. Their question troubled him so deeply that the aftershock was felt throughout the capital (Matt. 2:1–3).

Perhaps both parties were acquainted with the ancient prophecies of a coming kingdom—recorded in the oral traditions of the wise Easterners and written in part of the great book to which Herod paid such scant attention (Dan. 2:44–45), despite his easy access to it (cf. Matt. 2:4–6).

Some thirty years later, John the Baptist appeared in the wilderness of Judea, a latter-day Elijah proclaiming that this long-promised kingdom of God was already coming over the horizon of history. His message was both echoed by, and fulfilled in, his cousin Jesus of Nazareth: "Repent, for the kingdom of heaven/God is at hand" (Matt. 4:17; cf. Mark 1:14).

Now—at last—the kingdom was here; the King Himself had arrived.

But what does this mean—Jesus is King? Yes, Jesus came to be "King of my life," but the gospel story portrays a kingship simultaneously more deeply anchored in the history of God's revelation and more cosmic in its implications.

In fact, when Jesus first announced His kingdom and reign, two of its major events already lay in the past.

## *Anointed and Opposed*

First, He had been "Christ-ed," anointed into the office of King, by the powerful coming of the Holy Spirit on Him at His baptism in the River

Jordan (Luke 3:21–22). That pointed Him forward to the overwhelming baptism into death He would experience at Calvary (Luke 12:50). By that baptism of blood He would conquer sin, death, and Satan (Col. 2:13–15; Heb. 2:14–15).

But there was more to it than this. For, second, His baptism was followed by an immediate conflict. He went from the waters of Jordan to the wilderness of Judea to battle face to face with Satan himself (Luke 4:1–13). This event, perhaps even more clearly, set the parameters of His kingdom, because in it Jesus proved to be everything that both Adam and Israel had failed to be.

## Adam the First

Adam the First had been created in fellowship with God *as His image* (Gen. 1:26–27). In the ancient Near East, a king might symbolize his lordship over his territory by setting up an image as a representation of himself and his dominion. This is precisely what Genesis 1 describes: God, the Great King, made man as His living, breathing, moving, like-Himself image.

God gave Adam the First "dominion." He was to rule over the animate world (Gen. 1:26). In the context of his fellowship with God in Eden, he also was called to turn the whole earth into the garden of God (Gen. 1:28). In amazing and imaginative love, God fashioned a creature that, in miniature, could experience creativity and dominion, and so have real fellowship with Him.

Here lay the serpent's subtlety—"You will be like God" (Gen. 3:5), he intoned salaciously when he tempted the woman. He blinded her to the cardinal truth: *Adam and Eve already were like God; they were His image!*

So Adam the First fell, and with him the cosmos.

## Adam the Last

Enter Adam the Last. The Lord Jesus was anointed with the Spirit, who is both the Divine Reconnaissance Officer (He is "the seven Spirits of God *sent out into all the earth*," Rev. 5:6) and also the Divine Strategist (He leads the new Adam out to be tempted by the Devil, Matt. 4:1).

The replay of the battle for cosmic dominion did not take place in a garden, but in a wilderness created by sin. The animals that surrounded Jesus were not subservient and tranquil, but "wild" (Mark 1:13). Nevertheless, the temptations to which Adam the First fell (and Israel following him) were faced head on by Adam the Last, overcome successfully, and their author routed.

Jesus had come in order to establish His lordship over all things and to restore the reign of man over the earth. The prince of this world therefore offered its kingdoms to Jesus. But he did so in a way that would make Jesus *his* subject (Matt. 4:9). Thankfully, the prince of darkness and death was no match for the Prince of Light and Life. Anticipating the more bloody battle of the cross, Jesus stood firm.

Thus, in one Man, a foothold had been gained in enemy-occupied territory and a fatal flaw discovered in Satan's character, tactics, and resources. The kingdom had indeed come near.

No wonder our Lord's ministry then began with a proclamation of this good news and marvelous demonstrations of His power over disease, chaos in creation, and the Evil One himself (Mark 4:35–5:43).

### Climactic Battle

But a final battle for dominion remained to be fought. God had promised a day of bloody conflict between the Seed of the woman and the serpent. The heel of the woman's Seed would be crushed even as He crushed the head of the serpent (see Gen. 3:15). This was settled in the purpose of God from all ages (2 Tim. 1:9–10).

The Gospels describe how the antagonists moved irrevocably toward the final denouement. God's battle plan was in place. Satan, who earlier had sought to prevent the cross, desperately rushed to destroy the Son, God's King—and seemed to succeed. He who held the power of death had Adam the Last in his clutches on the cross.

But this was a King who died voluntarily, bearing the guilt of sins not His own. Truly, such a good Man can never be held down (Acts 2:24)!

Thus, Christ triumphed over Satan in the cross (Col. 2:15), and in His resurrection and ascension-coronation He received from the Father authority to give to all His people the same Spirit who had anointed Him (John 14:16; Acts 2:33). The Spirit of the King is poured out on His subjects so that "of the increase of His government and peace there will be no end" (Isa. 9:7). And so today men and women, boys and girls, young and old, rich and poor, wise and simple from all the world's tribes, tongues, peoples, and nations bow the knee to Him and call Him Lord.

## Consummation

We do not see everything under man's feet—not yet. But we see Jesus already crowned with glory and honor (Heb. 2:5–9a) because He tasted death for us (Heb. 2:9). We see Him by faith, and we realize that His enthroned presence in heaven is the guarantee that He will return to consummate the kingdom He already has inaugurated. Then the last word will be spoken; then the final reversal will take place. The new order begun in the resurrection of our King will spread to everything that He claims for Himself: the fissures in the created order will be sealed and transformed; the groans of creation will be heard no longer (Rom. 8:19–22). Everywhere and in everything there will be reflections of His perfect glory. Then loud voices in heaven will be heard saying, "The kingdoms of this world have become the kingdoms of our Lord and of His Christ, and He shall reign forever and ever!" (Rev. 11:15).

But all this lay in the future of the Little One wrapped in swaddling cloths in the Bethlehem manger (Luke 2:12). For the present, the One who "binds up the water in His thick clouds" (Job 26:8), the One who can "bind the cluster of the Pleiades" (Job 38:31), Himself lay bound in strips of cloth wrapped around Him under the illusion that otherwise His little limbs might become deformed in later life.[16]

Here are wonders upon wonders: the Strong One is weak; the Infinite One lies in a manger; the Prince of Life dies; the Crucified One lives; the Humiliated One is glorified.

Meekness and majesty, indeed!

Behold, then, your newborn King! Come and worship Him!

# 13

# YESTERDAY, TODAY, AND FOREVER

J esus Christ is the same yesterday, today, and forever" (Heb. 13:8) must be one of the most frequently de-contextualized texts in the entire New Testament.

Yes, it has all the essential ingredients for being treated as though it had fallen out of a fortune cookie instead of emerging from the carefully crafted teaching of Hebrews. There is no verb in the Greek text, but there are three self-evident points: yesterday, today, and forever.

However, here, as elsewhere, "every text has its context." This statement about the changelessness of Christ is not giving expression to a Platonic, timeless idea, but to a truth that emerges from the history of redemption.

For the author of Hebrews, the history of the people of God is one of pilgrimage to the heavenly Zion, typified by the exodus-wilderness wan-derings-entrance into the Promised Land experience of the Old Testament saints. Characteristic of God's dealings with His people then, as now, was the principle "Follow My leader" (Moses, Joshua, and others) until the people were brought from the darkness of the Egyptian past, through the struggles of their present pilgrimage, and into the anticipated blessings of the Promised Land.

In those circumstances, their faith always had three dimensions: on the basis of God's Word given yesterday, they lived as His redeemed people in the present, certain that He would keep His promises forever. This is the faith defined in Hebrews 11:1, illustrated in 11:3–40 by the heroes and heroines of the Old Testament, and fully exemplified in Jesus—faith's author and finisher, its supreme exemplar but also its object (Heb. 12:1–2).

In the old era, people followed and imitated such men and women of faith. So, too, in the new era. But in *both* cases, the eyes of believers are ultimately fixed on the person of Christ Himself. He is one and the same *yesterday* for them in the old epoch, *today* for us in the resurrection age (cf. Heb. 1:5; Acts 13:33), and *forever* for all believers in every age.

Three important implications are wrapped up in this great summary statement about Christ.

## *The Constancy of Christ*

Christ is always the same. Here at the end of his letter, the author echoes a theme from its beginning. "To the Son He says: . . . 'You [remain] the same'" (Heb. 1:8, 12, citing Ps. 102:27). But now he makes explicit what earlier was implicit. The immutable One of Psalm 102 is none other than the incarnate One of the gospel.

The practical implication of this becomes clear when we remember that Psalm 102 is possibly the most eloquent description of depression and despair to be found in the entire Psalter. The psalmist's mental salvation lay in his rediscovery of the immutability of God. Hebrews gives that truth flesh-and-blood dimensions in Jesus Christ. You can trust Him; He is always the same.

Do not mistake the meaning. This is not the immutability of the sphinx—a Christ captured once for all in a never-fading still photograph. This is the changelessness of Jesus Christ in all His life, love, holiness, grace, justice, truth, and power. He is always the same for you, no matter how your circumstances change.

Say this to yourself when you rise each day, when you struggle, or when you lay your head down sadly on your pillow at night: "Lord Jesus, You are still the same, and always will be."

## *The Importance of the Gospels*

The immutability of Christ is the changelessness of the Christ revealed in the Gospels. All that He proved to be in His ministry is an indication of the way He really and always is. That is why it is legitimate for us to see the Gospel accounts not only in the context of redemptive history but as portrayals of the character of the Christ who lives forever. We are able to say, "If Jesus was like this *then*, Jesus is like this *now*."

Do you know the Christ of the Gospels? Or have you fallen into the trap to which Christians (especially, perhaps, Reformed Christians) who love doctrine and systematic theology are sometimes susceptible (unlike John Calvin, it should be said): fascination with dogmatic formula at the expense of love for the Savior's person?

## *The Touchstone of Truth*

It is not accidental that Hebrews' words about Christ are followed by an exhortation not to be "carried away by all kinds of strange teachings" (13:9, NIV).

False teaching, be it doctrinal or ethical, always will have the effect of making us "major on minors," obscuring from us the central glory of the Lord Jesus Himself. We cannot always easily articulate what is wrong with such influences. But the context suggests we should ask: "Is this teaching by which I am being influenced leading me to love and trust Jesus Christ more? Or less? Have I exchanged communion with Christ for caviling about incidentals?"

By the same token, growing in faith and love for Christ, revealed as He is in Scripture, will be the greatest of all preservatives against being led astray. The person who is saturated in the teaching and spirit of the Gospels will have his or her senses "trained . . . to distinguish good from evil" (Heb. 5:14, NIV) and to know what is truly Christ-like and Christ-honoring. That, too, is an implication of knowing that "Jesus Christ is the same yesterday, today, and forever."

From first to last, then, fix your eyes on Christ. He never changes!

# 14

# THE RESURRECTION
# AND THE LIFE

he Gospel records of Jesus' ministry tell us of only three people He raised from the dead, although there may have been more (Matt. 11:4–5). Only the daughter of Jairus and the son of the widow of Nain feature in the first three Gospels. These are wonderful events, but they are not portrayed as turning points in Jesus' ministry.

By contrast, when John describes the raising of Lazarus (the only incident of its kind that he records), the critical significance of the event is underlined: "Jesus said, 'This sickness will not end in death. No, it is for God's glory so that God's Son may be glorified through it'" (John 11:4, NIV).

In fact, Jesus delayed going to Bethany because the death and restoration of Lazarus were integral elements in the path to His glorification, which, in John, takes place through His death (12:23). Significantly, the raising of Lazarus is bracketed by Thomas's unintended prophecy of Jesus' death (11:16) and the plots hatched within the Sanhedrin to bring it about (11:45–57; 12:9–11).

The raising of Lazarus is the seventh and last miracle in John's "Book of Signs" (John 1–12). It marks the climax to which everything has led. It points to the ultimate miracle of the "Book of Glory" (John 13–21), that is, the resurrection of our Lord, God, and Savior (John 20:31).

What does it teach us about Him? Note these three truths:

## *True Humanity*

Here we catch sight of the true, deep humanity of Jesus. Attention is often drawn to the words of the Bible's shortest verse: "Jesus wept" (11:35). Those tears reveal an earthquake of emotions in Jesus' heart. "He was deeply moved in spirit and troubled" (11:33, NIV) is a correct but scarcely adequate translation of words that express the deep inner disturbance and anger of our Lord in the face of Satan's reign in sin and death.

Jesus' sinlessness should not be equated with emotionlessness. The opposite is nearer the truth. His holy humanity experienced heights and depths of emotion unknown by sinful humanity. Seeing human need with perfect clarity, Jesus felt it with unparalleled intensity. Our senses, by comparison, are numbed. Thus, the crisis of the death of Lazarus—whom Jesus loved—became the occasion for a yet fuller revelation of the sensitivity of our Lord's holy humanity (Heb. 2:10–11, 14–18; 4:14–16).

## *Jesus' Power*

Jesus also reveals His power to give life to the dead. With one command, "Lazarus, come forth!" (11:43), He raised His dead friend.

It is fascinating to notice that our Lord accomplished this by two means: prayer and His word (vv. 41–43). He is the Ezekiel-like prophet who speaks both to the bones and the spirits of those who have fallen prey to the curse of sin. He brings new life to the dead. What the prophets of God did spiritually, the Prophet of God did quite literally and physically.

The emphasis on prayer here should not go unnoticed—the apostles certainly grasped it (Acts 6:4). In addition, a pattern is illustrated that is characteristic of Christ's ongoing activity as the giver of new life: resurrection comes by His spoken word.

This has often puzzled theologians. The gift of new life is a sovereign act of God. It is monergistic, not synergistic, in character. God alone is the agent; we do not cooperate in receiving new life. Yet, according to Scripture, it is through the Word of God that we receive this new life (James 1:18; 1 Peter 1:23).

**Question**: Surely the instrumentality of the Word (to which we actively respond) implies an activity on our part? Do we not, in this sense, contribute something to being born anew?

**Answer**: No more than Jesus' command implies that Lazarus contributes life energy to his own resurrection. Lazarus comes out of the tomb because Jesus raises him from the dead, not in order that he might be raised from the dead. In him, our Lord's words are fulfilled: "Most assuredly, I say to you, the hour is coming, and now is, when the dead will hear the voice of the Son of God; and those who hear will live" (John 5:25). When prayer to the Father and the word of command to the dead come from the lips of Jesus, His voice opens deaf ears and raises the dead.

What was true then remains so now (which is why we join prayer and preaching), and will continue to be at the last, when by His powerful command Christ once again will raise the dead (1 Thess. 4:16). In undiluted monergism, He called the galaxies into being, and He gives life to the dead in the same way (Rom. 4:17).

### Consummation

Here, too, is a glimpse of the purpose of Jesus in consummating His kingdom.

John's Gospel speaks of Jesus' miracles as "signs." Signs are often miniature, even coded, representations of the reality to which they point. So they are here. For a moment, Jesus, the Light of the World (John 8:12; 1:5), shines in a way that irresistibly overcomes the world's darkness, and says, "This is who I am and this is what I will do."

One day Christ will return in the full glory of His resurrection power. The light will be switched on permanently. The Lamb of God who took away the sin of the world will be present in the new heavens and earth as their lamp. Neither sun nor moon will be needed (Rev. 21:23). As He will be the Life, so He will be the Light of the new world.

"Jesus said to her, 'I am the resurrection and the life. He who believes in Me, though he may die, he shall live. . . . Do you believe this?'" (John 11:25–26).

Well, do you?

PART III

# The Spirit
# of Christ

*Growing in grace involves both knowledge and the experience of the Spirit's life-transforming ministry. This is what the New Testament means when it speaks about "the communion of the Holy Spirit" (2 Cor. 13:14).*

# 15

# THE GREAT FEAST

D aily throughout the weeklong Feast of Tabernacles (John 7), the pilgrims crowding Jerusalem had witnessed a thrilling spectacle. Picture the scene:

The high priest filled a golden pitcher with water from the Pool of Siloam and carried it in procession to the temple. There, the ceremonial trumpet was blown and the priests walked around the altar. As they did so, the choir sang Psalms 113–118. As they began to sing Psalm 118, the pilgrims raised aloft thin bundles of sticks and shouted "Thanks be to God" over and over. The water then was poured out in a thank offering to the Lord.

What an occasion. The ceremony offered a foretaste of the messianic blessings for which the thirsty people of God longed. Surely God's promise would be fulfilled soon, for had He not said, "With joy you will draw water from the wells of salvation" (Isa. 12:3)?

On the last day of the feast, the "great day" (7:37)—perhaps the day when all fell quiet, since this scene was not reenacted—Jesus urges those in the temple precincts to come to Him, promising that He will quench their thirst:

*On the last day, that great day of the feast, Jesus stood and cried out, saying, "If anyone thirsts, let him come to Me and drink. He who believes in Me, as the Scripture has said, out of his heart will flow rivers of living water." But this He spoke concerning the Spirit, whom those believing in Him would receive; for the Holy Spirit was not yet given, because Jesus was not yet glorified.*

—JOHN 7:37–39

## A Startling Statement

Jesus is referring to the gift of the Spirit that believers will receive later. But John adds a strange explanatory statement: "The Holy Spirit was not yet given [literally: "not yet was the Spirit"], because Jesus was not yet glorified."

Why does John express himself in this startling way? Because he wants to underline the privilege of new covenant believers; they experience something no old covenant believer could.

But what?

One clue lies in the link John makes between the gift of the Spirit and the glorifying of Jesus (v. 39). Although there are previous references in John's Gospel to the "glory" of Jesus (cf. 1:14; 2:11), this is the first of a series of references to Him being glorified through His death, burial, and resurrection. The manner in which believers are to receive the Spirit depends, apparently, on Jesus' work being finished. Then the Spirit will come in a new capacity—then streams of living water will flow from within (v. 38).

## The River Source

Most modern versions of the Bible indicate in a footnote that there is some difficulty in understanding and translating these words. That is partly because the earliest manuscripts of the New Testament did not use modern punctuation. It is also not obvious what Scripture passage Jesus is referencing when He says, "*As the Scripture has said,* out of his heart will flow rivers of living water" (v. 38); no verse says this directly.

A glance at two possible translations of vv. 37–38 clarifies the issue:

### Primary ESV translation:

On the last day of the feast, the great day, Jesus stood up and cried out, "If anyone thirsts, let him come to me and drink. Whoever believes in me, as the Scripture has said, 'Out of his heart will flow rivers of living water.'"

**Alternative ESV translation:**

On the last day of the feast, the great day, Jesus stood up and cried out, "If anyone thirsts, let him come to me, and let him who believes in me drink. As the Scripture has said, 'Out of his heart will flow rivers of living water.'"

If the first translation is correct, then it is possible that the rivers of living water (the Holy Spirit) are viewed as flowing from within the believer. But in the alternative translation, the rivers, i.e. the Spirit, flow from Christ Himself to the believer. Does Jesus mean that the rivers of living water will come from within the believer or from within Himself?

In either case, the Christian believer receives, experiences, and enjoys the Spirit. But if the reference here is to Jesus as the source of the living water, these words express remarkable teaching on the Spirit's ministry. For then John is helping his readers to understand that it is from the glorified Jesus that the Spirit flows: "But this He spoke concerning the Spirit, whom those believing in Him would receive; for the Holy Spirit was not yet given, because Jesus was not yet glorified."

There seem to be good reasons for believing this is what John is saying.

Earlier, in John 4:13–14, Jesus said He is the One who gives the living water of the Spirit.

Well-known Old Testament passages would then lie behind the statement that the Scriptures would be fulfilled:

1. The descriptions of Moses smiting the rock from which water rushed (Ex. 17:1–7; Num. 20:1–13).

2. Ezekiel's vision of the new temple to which God's glory returned (Ezek. 43:1–5) and from which rivers flowed (Ezek. 47:1–12).

Perhaps both are in the background here. Jesus is the smitten Rock (1 Cor. 10:3–4). It is from the smitten Lord that the Spirit is given to us. Is this why John pointedly mentions that when Jesus' side was pierced, water as well as blood flowed (John 19:34)?

Jesus is also the temple to which glory returns (John 1:14). He is resurrected as the true tabernacle-temple in whom God's glory is restored. It is from within Him, risen and glorified, that the Spirit comes to the disciples in the symbolism of Jesus' breath (John 20:22).

## So What?

This is a poignant portrayal of the gift of the Spirit from the resurrected Lord. Furthermore, it is in keeping with the rest of the New Testament's teaching (cf. Acts 2:33).

But does this make any difference to us? Indeed it does, for it implies that Jesus bore the Spirit throughout His life in order to give us the same Spirit He bore. The Spirit He gives to us is the very same Spirit who accompanied and sustained our Lord Jesus throughout the whole of His ministry.

William Still, my minister during my student days in Scotland, used to urge us to meditate on these penetrating words:

> *Think what Spirit dwells within thee,*
> *What a Father's smile is thine,*
> *What thy Savior died to win thee;*
> *Child of heaven, should'st thou repine?*[17]

Has it dawned on you just who is the Spirit who dwells within you? He is the Spirit of the smitten Rock and the New Temple. As you read through John's Gospel, reflect on this: at every juncture of Jesus' ministry, the Spirit is able to say, "Been there, done that."

It is this Spirit who indwells me if, in my thirst, I have come to Christ and begun to drink.

Awesome indeed!

# 16

# THE HOLY SPIRIT

Bible translations are in the news these days, sometimes for controversial reasons. But one universal benefit of modern translations is that the Holy Spirit is no longer referred to as "it" as He often was in earlier generations. Curiously, the chief culprit here was probably the much-loved King James Version of the Bible (e.g., Rom. 8:26, "The Spirit *itself . . .*").

The Greek word for Spirit (*pneuma*) is a neuter gender noun, so it attracted a neuter pronoun ("it"). But such passages as John 14:26 ("He will teach") and 15:26 ("He will testify") use the masculine pronoun to refer to the Spirit and leave us in no doubt about His personal nature. The Spirit is "He," not "it."

As the early fathers of the Christian church understood, whatever it means for us as humans to be "personal" beings mirrors the personal being of God—in miniature, one might say. God possesses personal being in a unified, uncreated, eternal, tri-personal manner. We are created in a mono-personal manner. We are a tiny reflection of God, the great triune original.

### *Holy* Spirit?

But what does Scripture mean when it speaks of God as Father, Son, and *Spirit*?

The Old Testament word for spirit, *ruach*, is an onomatopoeic word. It expresses its meaning partly by its sound. *Ruach* means, basically, wind in motion, sometimes storm wind. It denotes the expressing of power (cf. the parallelism in Micah 3:8, "I am filled with *power*, with the *Spirit* of the Lord, and with justice and *might*"; NIV, emphasis added). In that sense, *ruach* also can be used to describe the driving characteristic of an individual (he or she is "sweet," "mean," or "high-spirited").

But on occasion, *ruach* is set in parallelism with the "face" of God (Ps. 104:29–30; Ezek. 39:29), conveying the multi-dimensional sense of presence, revelation, knowledge, provision, and communion. The great Aaronic blessing—"The Lord bless you and keep you; the Lord make His *face* to shine upon you . . . the Lord lift up His countenance [*face*] upon you" (Num. 6:24–26, emphasis added)—in its own way expressed the covenant ministry of the Holy Spirit. This is how God "put His name upon" His old covenant people (Num. 6:27). In the same way, in baptism, the Lord puts the same name on His new covenant people—only that name is now pronounced "Father, Son, and Holy Spirit" (Matt. 28:18–20).

It lies on the surface of the Bible, therefore, that the Holy Spirit is:

1. Divine, because the attributes and actions of God are ascribed to Him.
2. Personal, because these attributes and activities are personal in nature.

Yet is there not something about this name—*Spirit*—that suggests the elusive? Did not Jesus Himself say, with reference to the Spirit, that the wind (*pneuma*) blows where it wills, but we cannot tell where it comes from or goes (John 3:8)? And are we not treading on dangerous ground if we inquire further about the identity of the Spirit when Jesus stressed that the Spirit does not glorify Himself (John 16:14)?

## *Focus on the Spirit?*

The humility of the Spirit in relationship to the work of the Son is not a reason to inquire no further about His own person and character. After all, if we love a modest person, we want to know all we possibly can about that person and to praise him or her! Similarly, the ministry of the Spirit in honoring the Lord Jesus simply underlines the responsibility of the church to know Him, love Him, and adore Him for who He is—God Himself. It was for this that the great Cappadocian father Gregory of Nyssa[18] battled in the wake of the Arian controversy—that the Spirit should be "with the Father and the Son together . . . worshiped and glorified" (Nicene-Constantinopolitan Creed, AD 381).

But we cannot offer true worship to Him unless we know Him. And only when we know Him does "the communion of the Holy Spirit" (2 Cor. 13:14) become a reality to us. But how can we "know" Him when He seems to be so faceless, when even His name lacks the personal connotations of either "Father" or "Son"?

Meditation on two aspects of the Bible's teaching may help us here.

### Another Like Jesus

First, the Scriptures use a whole series of descriptions to help us identify the Spirit. He is the Spirit of grace, of holiness, of glory, of sonship—and much more. Perhaps most significantly, we should notice how our Lord introduces Him in His Farewell Discourse (John 14–16). Jesus tells His disciples that the Spirit will be to them everything that He Himself already has been during the course of His ministry.

Jesus promises to send the Spirit as "another Helper" (John 14:16). Our English word *another* can mean two things—"another of the same kind" or "another of a different kind." The Greek language has different words for these ideas. Here, "another" translates the Greek *allos*, which in this context means "another of the same kind." The Spirit is a Helper just like Jesus!

### Jesus and the Spirit

While the Son and the Spirit are personally distinct, they are entwined with one another. Jesus is Teacher, Jesus is Guide, Jesus is Counselor, Jesus goes to make a home for His disciples. The Spirit is another like Jesus: He teaches, guides, counsels, and brings orphans into the home and heart of God. Moreover, because He is Spirit, He does this by personally indwelling our spirits in a mysterious yet wonderfully real and powerful way.

This is why it was an advantage for the disciples (and us!) that Jesus should leave (John 16:7). Their fear was that they would lose Jesus and that their years of intimate knowledge and fellowship would come to nothing. The truth was that they would come to know Him better. They would be bound to Him with an intimacy that only the divine Spirit could give because the Spirit was with and on the Lord Jesus throughout all the years of His life and ministry.

All this, of course, belongs to what theologians call the "economic" ministry of the Spirit—His work in the created world. Behind that ministry lies the union and fellowship of the Spirit with the Father and the Son.

Is this relationship simply a dark, never-to-be-known secret? By no means, for God's revelation truly is a revelation, a personal unveiling of Himself. He is not different from who He reveals Himself to be. Yes, our understanding is creaturely and limited; yet, even finite knowledge of the true God is still true knowledge.

## In the Life of God

What, then, does Scripture teach us about the being and inner-Trinitarian life of the Spirit?

There are several wonderful things we can learn. Here are only a few:

The Spirit knows God the Father and God the Son down to the very depths of Their personal being in the Godhead. He searches "the deep things of God" (1 Cor. 2:10). Thus, between the Spirit and the Father, between the Spirit and the Son, there is total mutual understanding and knowledge. Nothing is hidden. More than that, all that is in both the Father and the Son is embraced and received by the Spirit, as though He drinks eternally and infinitely of the glory of the divine attributes expressed in each of these persons.

In addition, nothing about the mutual relationship of the Father and the Son is hidden from the Spirit. Their mutual devotion, the expressions of all of Their personal attributes to each other, is not to the exclusion of the Spirit, as though He were an outsider. On the contrary, part of the mutual delight of Father and Son, in pouring all that each of Them is into the other, is that in Their doing so the Spirit experiences not only what each is in Himself, but also this added dimension of what each is to the other.

All this lies behind the remarkable words of Jesus when He promises that (after His death, resurrection, and ascension) He will ask the Father to send the Spirit. He describes Him as One who "proceeds from the Father" (15:26). The sending from the Father and the Son was economic (still future tense); the proceeding, however, appears to be perennial, not bounded by the past or by the future. The Spirit always "goes out from" the Father, not in the sense of depending on the Father for His being, but finding in the Father the deep things of His relationship with the Son. Here His activity is described in terms of its voluntariness rather than its submissiveness (He "goes out" of His own accord, but He is "sent" by the Father in the name of the Son).

When we speak of this we realize that we are stretching our minds to the limits; we are saying things we do not understand fully. But as our intellects stand on tiptoe, stretching to grasp the far horizons of divine revelation, we are not distressed by the limitations on our understanding. Rather, we are on the stretch in adoration and awe, "lost in wonder, love and praise."[19]

Paradoxically, it is by the Spirit's shining on the face of Christ, and by the Son's leading us to the Father, that we begin to realize who He is who has conducted us into this fellowship. With the apostle John (1 John 1:3), we turn to the Spirit who has brought us to see this glory and say, "Surely, blessed Spirit, You have brought us into the fellowship of the Father and His Son, Jesus Christ the Righteous One."

# 17

# WHEN THE
# SPIRIT COMES

Jesus' Farewell Discourse (John 14–16) forms the centerpiece of the upper room narrative (John 13–17) and has rightly been described as a casket of spiritual jewels.

But Christians have sometimes been overly hasty in interpreting parts of these chapters. We tend to bypass the historical context of Jesus' words and treat them as though they were timeless truths spoken directly to us.

These chapters are, of course, highly profitable to us for doctrine, reproof, correction, and training in righteousness, like all Scripture (2 Tim. 3:16–17)—but only, surely, as rightly interpreted.

Take one example of over-hasty interpretation: Jesus promises that the Spirit will teach the apostles all things, remind them of everything He has said, show them things to come, and guide them into all the truth (John 14:26; 16:12–13). This is frequently read as if it were a promise given directly to us. But this is to bypass the context, for here Jesus is speaking to the apostles (not directly to us!). He is specifically promising them that they will be vehicles of new revelation that will, eventually, constitute the New Testament Scriptures.

A similar example is Jesus' promise that when the Spirit comes He will engage in a threefold ministry of conviction in relation to sin, righteousness, and judgment (John 16:8–11). Of course these words are relevant to the Spirit's present ministry. But we miss their rich significance if we interpret them in a way that bypasses their historical context. In their original setting, these words constitute a prophecy of the Spirit's work on the Day of Pentecost (Acts 2:1ff).

When we recognize this, we are able to fill out the content of the promise. But when we fail to recognize it, we are in danger of interpreting (and thus remolding and distorting) Scripture in the light of our own experience.

Jesus says the Spirit will "convict." This verb means anything from "pour contempt on" to "convince." This work has three dimensions to it: conviction of sin, righteousness, and judgment. But what does this mean? Jesus explains, and the events of Pentecost exemplify His answer.

## Convicted of Sin

First of all, the Spirit convinces of sin because men do not believe in Christ (John 16:9).

This does not mean that men are sinners *because* they do not believe in Christ. Rather, when the Spirit later came at Pentecost and brought glory to Christ in Peter's exaltation of him (Acts 2:22), his hearers realized their sin: Jesus was the Christ, and yet they had not believed in him. This was the specific sin of which they were convicted.

## Convicted of Righteousness

Second, the Spirit convinces of righteousness, because Jesus goes to the Father (John 16:10).

What is the connection between Christ's going to the Father and this conviction of righteousness?

In John's terminology, Jesus' "going to the Father" denotes the many-sided event of His death, resurrection, ascension, and exaltation at the Father's right hand. In the resurrection and its consequences, our Lord was divinely vindicated (cf. Rom. 1:4). He was proved to be the Righteous One, as Peter argued with great power at Pentecost.

But if Jesus was vindicated as the *Righteous* One, those who despised, rejected, and crucified Him were thereby condemned as unrighteous. They were thus convicted of His righteousness, their own lack of righteousness, and—wonder of all wonders—that, in the Righteous One whom they crucified, God provides righteousness for the unrighteous.

## Convicted of Judgment

Third, the Spirit convinces of judgment, because the prince of this world now stands condemned (John 16:11).

Once again, the events of Pentecost clarify what this means. Here were the men who had despised the whisper in their consciences that they were doing evil by ridding the world of Jesus. But on the cross Christ had judged and condemned the powers of darkness (John 12:31). The judgment meted against Him outside Jerusalem had been reversed when He walked out of the garden tomb. The implication could not be missed. If He had been condemned in error, then those who had condemned Him now stood condemned by the God who had raised Jesus from the dead.

Consider this idea carefully. The message the Spirit taught in the light of the resurrection was this: "Jesus was *not* guilty; therefore, you *are* guilty. And so now you, not Jesus, are arraigned before God's judgment, tried, and condemned!"

When the Spirit came at Pentecost, men and women were convicted of their sin and unbelief (Acts 2:23, 36); they were persuaded of the righteousness of the divinely vindicated Christ (Acts 2:24, 32–36); and they recognized His exaltation as Lord and felt their own perilous condition (Acts 2:34, 37).

## Lessons to Learn

What important lessons should we learn from this? Many, surely, but a vital one is that the truest, best, and deepest conviction is that which shows us two things:

First, that as sinners we need Christ.

Second, that the Christ we need is offered to us in the gospel.

Guilt can turn us to despair or to a new hard-heartedness. But true conviction turns us to Christ and to what is symbolized in baptism: your sins may be forgiven (Acts 2:38).

# 18

# SEEING JESUS— AT PENTECOST

T ry this simple word-association test. Write down the words you associate with the following terms: "Sinai," "Bethlehem," "Calvary," and "Pentecost."

Chances are that your responses to the first three are variants of "law" or "Moses," "birth of Jesus" or "manger," and "cross" or "crucifixion." However, you win a theology prize if you responded to "Pentecost" by saying "Jesus."

But isn't Pentecost about the Holy Spirit? To say "Jesus" might seem to many Christians as inappropriate as saying "Holy Spirit" in response to "Calvary." And yet, there is an important sense in which the scriptural account of the Day of Pentecost is intended to tell us more about Jesus than about the Holy Spirit.

We might have been able to work this out *a priori*, in view of what our Lord taught us the Spirit delights to do, namely to bring glory to Christ rather than to Himself (John 16:13–14). The opening words of Acts underline this. They hint that the entire book records not what the apostles or the Spirit did, but what Jesus continued to do, albeit that Jesus did it through the apostles in the power of the Spirit.

How does the coming of the Spirit at Pentecost floodlight the work of Jesus? There are several ways.

## *Enthronement*

First, the events of Pentecost provide the proof of the hidden enthronement of Jesus. The first logical deduction Peter's hearers needed to draw from this event was this: "Therefore let all the house of Israel know assuredly that God has made this Jesus, whom you crucified, both Lord and Christ" (Acts 2:36). Was Jesus not always Lord and Christ? Yes, but now He had entered into the triumph those titles suggest. How do we know? Because the gift of the Spirit had been poured out.

The ethos of this reasoning may be missed by citizens of the United States, who experience presidential inaugurations but never royal coronations! I am old enough (just!) to remember the coronation of the present Queen Elizabeth. To celebrate her enthronement, all the children throughout her realm were given a gift. It was the celebratory sign of her coronation.

The same is true here. Our Lord Jesus has been enthroned as King in glory. But that enthronement cannot be seen at present. How, then, can we be sure it has taken place, the kingdom has been inaugurated, and the last days of the present age have therefore come? The outpouring of the gift of the Spirit on all of God's children (Acts 2:17–18) is the assurance that Jesus is King!

## *Behind Closed Doors*

But second, the coming of the Spirit indicated that a heavenly transaction had taken place between the Son and the Father. The often-overlooked words of Acts 2:33 record it: "being exalted to the right hand of God, and having received from the Father the promise of the Holy Spirit. . . ."

Here, momentarily, a door into heaven is opened and we are given a glimpse into the fellowship between the Son and the Father. The ascended Son comes to the Father. What will He say? "Father, do you remember what you promised the Great King? You said, 'Ask of Me, and I will give You the nations for Your inheritance, and the ends of the earth for Your possession' (Ps. 2:8). You said about the Suffering Servant: 'Behold, My Servant. . . . Kings shall shut their mouths at Him. . . . He shall see His seed, He shall prolong His days, and the pleasure of the LORD shall prosper in His hand. . . . I will divide Him a portion with the great, and He shall divide the spoil with the strong, because He poured out His soul unto death . . .' (Isa. 52:13, 15; 53:10, 12). Father, fulfill Your promises to Me."

How was this worldwide dominion to be established? All authority now belonged to Jesus. He had promised that the disciples would receive the Holy Spirit and He would give them power to be witnesses in Jerusalem, Judea, Samaria, and then to the ends of the earth. The disciples, therefore, would go into all the world proclaiming Jesus. He would be with them to the end—through the presence of the Spirit-witness.

## Firstfruits

Third, Pentecost was the firstfruits of the fulfillment of Jesus' own promise about the ministry of the Spirit: "And when He has come, He will convict the world of sin, and of righteousness, and of judgment" (John 16:8). Jesus' own explanation of this is illuminating. The Spirit will convict the world "of sin, because they do not believe in Me; of righteousness, because I go to My Father and you see Me no more; of judgment, because the ruler of this world is judged" (John 16:9–11). The conviction mentioned in this promise is related to the way the Spirit reveals Jesus Himself. The Spirit makes it evident that He is the Messiah, the Son of the Father to whom He has returned, the One who defeated Satan by defeating death as the wages of sin. From first to last, then, the Spirit says, "Jesus."

Is there any pastoral value to this biblical theology? Yes, indeed. One hundred and twenty men and women were full of Christ. They were overwhelmed with a sense of His exaltation and enthronement, absolutely assured that He is reigning and will reign throughout the world. They had a heartfelt certainty that if God had kept this, the greatest of His promises, He would keep all of His promises.

Somewhere along the line, many Christians have lost this sense of the exaltation, enthronement, and triumph of Christ. We need to grasp that Jesus' coronation has taken place. He is already enthroned. That is why we are to go into the world with the good news—in the power of the Holy Spirit.

# 19

# THE PROMISE
# OF POWER

We are all very church-conscious these days. In many respects, that is a healthy thing, for evangelicalism has sometimes been over-obsessed with individual conversion and parachurch structures while being weak on the doctrine and practice of church life. By contrast, Jesus' vision was church-centered. He said, "I will build My church . . ." (Matt. 16:18).

Today there is a plethora of literature on the church—mainly of a pragmatic kind. From this smorgasbord, one can select anything from user-friendly to purpose-driven to we-at-least-do-it-right manuals.

It is characteristic of distinctively *Reformed* Christians to regard these trends with a jaundiced eye. Reformed believers tend to have a better-than-average sense of church history. We have seen it all—or at least read some of it—before.

All this makes one wonder about the promise of Jesus to the apostles: when the Holy Spirit comes, He said, "you shall receive power [*dunamis*] . . . and you shall be witnesses to Me" (Acts 1:8). They obeyed His command to "tarry in the city of Jerusalem" and were indeed "endued with power [*dunamis*] from on high" (Luke 24:49). The rest, as they say, is history. A roomful of people (120 of them, according to Acts 1:15) would soon turn the world upside down.

## *Is There an Explanation?*

Is the explanation for these events simply that, in those frequently overlooked weeks between the resurrection and the ascension, our Lord was providing His own seminar on kingdom expansion (Acts 1:3)?

The transformation of the disciples from a small group huddling together in a room in fear to a band of bold witnesses for Christ would never have taken place apart from the resurrection. And the weeks of teaching that followed, when He instructed them about the kingdom of God, obviously played a key role.

But all this came to fruition only when the Holy Spirit came. When *Christ* was with them, the disciples received instruction. But only when the *Holy Spirit* came upon them did they receive the power (*dunamis*) they needed to witness to Him ("you shall receive power *when the Holy Spirit has come*").

Isn't this what is missing—power? We lack power for witness.

## *Once-for-All Pentecost?*

Some who read these words may perhaps smile at their apparent theological naïveté. They know that Pentecost was a once-for-all event in redemptive history, one that was not intended to be a paradigm for Christian experience.

Yes, indeed. But that does not turn Pentecost into an event in a quasi-Platonic sphere. Redemptive history is real history, earth history; the participants at Pentecost actually experienced what is described. Not only so, but elements of that experience were repeated in their lives and manifested as well in the lives of others.

The element of power for witness was an experiential reality in the lives of the early disciples. Furthermore, the filling of the Spirit on the Day of Pentecost (Acts 2:4) was repeated (Acts 4:8, 31; 13:9). And certainly the evidences of similar power are spread throughout the New Testament (e.g., 1 Thess. 1:6–8). Paul himself sees such experiences in part as an answer to prayer for a specific enabling to speak the gospel fully and boldly (Eph. 6:18–19).

The apostles saw that Pentecost was a once-for-all-time, epoch-making event, but with often-repeatable elements built into it. The empowering for witness that Jesus promised was to be limited neither to the single event of Pentecost nor exclusively to the apostles. It extended beyond their persons and time (Acts. 2:4).

## A Word to the Reformed

This is what we still need: power to witness. The truth is that nothing would as readily silence gainsayers against the Reformed faith as would this. Far more important, it is only through such empowering that we will get beyond witnessing to fellow Christians about the Reformed faith and start witnessing to non-Christians about saving faith.

Looking over the past several decades, Reformed Christians have a great deal in which to rejoice. From a human perspective, it is probable that many readers of this book never would have discovered Reformed theology fifty years ago. The media through which we have learned it were almost non-existent. Reformed magazines and books were known to only a few cognoscenti. Few pulpits, and fewer conferences, were marked by its convictions. We can rejoice in the outpouring of riches we have received. As a result of it, the Reformed community has been growing exponentially worldwide.

But growth sometimes turns out to be a kind of ecclesiastical musical chairs. We need to exemplify something much richer than that—in impact on the ungodly world. That requires power in witness.

## Power through Fellowship

How do we "receive power"? It is the fruit not merely of book learning but of Christ fellowshiping—being more with Him, engaging in serious intercession in His name, meditating more on His glories. Perhaps in our much studying and discussing we have lost the biblical art of "waiting" and are all too prone to run ahead when the Spirit has not sent us with His anointing.

But another crucial thing is required here. Those who received such power in the apostolic days had to settle the related issue of crucifixion. They grasped that the risen Lord was the One who had first become a crucified Savior. Following Him meant a mark across their shoulders, a piercing of their hands and feet, and, yes, a gashing of their sides, too. *Waiting* without *emptying* will not lead to *going* with the *fullness* of the Spirit.

The lives that generally have been marked by power to witness have always been thus.

So, how about the *empowered* Reformed church? How about the *Spirit-filled* Reformed church? Is the Reformed church these things by definition? Only if there is first the *crucified* Reformed church.

# A HIDDEN REVIVAL

J onathan Edwards believed that God usually advances His kingdom through seasons of revival. He thus halts opposition to the gospel, brings conviction of sin, and builds the church. Here is how Edwards expressed it:

> It may here be observed, that from the fall of man to our day, the work of redemption in its effect has mainly been carried on by remarkable communications of the Spirit of God. Though there be a more constant influence of God's Spirit always in some degree attending his ordinances, yet the way in which the greatest things have been done towards carrying on this work, always have been by remarkable effusions, at special seasons of mercy.[20]

Whether we agree with Edwards' precise analysis or not, most of us recognize that there is something distinctive about what God did in the days of Edwards and George Whitefield. There was a "Great Awakening."

We think less often about the Reformation as a revival. And we rarely associate the names of Martin Luther and John Calvin with revival. But a great awakening the Reformation was, when unnumbered multitudes of people flocked to Christ under the new preaching of the gospel.

### *Revival in Palestine*

We think even less frequently of the days of awakening that surrounded the ministries of John the Baptist, then of Jesus, and later of the apostles. But around AD 30, days of remarkable spiritual awakening were witnessed in Palestine. John's Gospel gives us a series of hints to this effect.

Such was the impact of John the Baptist's ministry that end-of-the-world-type questions were being asked (John 1:19–23) and "people were constantly coming to be baptized" by John (3:23, NIV). Soon many believed in Jesus (2:23), so many that the word on the street was that Jesus had even more disciples than John (4:1).

During the early part of our Lord's ministry, this phenomenon continued. Jesus preached to crowds of five thousand families (6:10, where the number of men presumably represents family groups). Apparently many of them stayed overnight, sleeping rough, hoping for more (6:22). Revival days!

### *Revival When It Was Least Expected*

There was, however, one location in which the awakening was so wonderful that John pauses to describe it for us in detail. It was not in Galilee or in Jerusalem. What is so extraordinary about it is that it began with *one woman*, and the site was—of all places—*Sychar, Samaria* (John 4:3–42).

Here we are given both an example and a theology of revival.

What do we learn?

First, spiritual awakening takes place when Jesus Christ visits in saving power, in His sovereign time, and in His chosen way (4:4). No notice was posted at Jacob's Well announcing "Revival Week Here, Beginning Sunday!"

Second, Christ does not need the powerful and influential in order to reach a whole community. Deep conviction, thorough conversion, open confession—illustrated in the anonymous woman Jesus met at Jacob's Well—are His chosen instruments. The essential thing is not worldly greatness but the power of God evidenced in spiritual newness.

One Samaritan woman was Christ's human bridge into the entire Sychar community. Her fruitfulness was the consequence of a visitation of the Spirit—as it has often been in times of awakening. As in Jonah's record of revival (Jonah 3:4–5), her words of testimony were brief, but their impact was enormous. As Robert Murray McCheyne (who could speak from personal experience of being such an instrument) put it, "It is not much speaking, but much faith, that is needed."[21]

## The Secret

Our Lord took His disciples behind the scenes of this event to show them its secret. It was harvest time and they were to be reapers. But behind the harvest lies the plow; before the reaper comes the sower. Others had done the "labors" (4:38).

Who were the "others" mentioned in verse 38? Were there hidden ones in Sychar's past who had served Yahweh faithfully in a spiritually compromised society?

Certainly Jesus Himself, the sent-One of the Father, plowed deeply and patiently by the power of the Spirit into one individual's life. That one life, well-plowed, sown with gospel seed, bearing a harvest, was His instrument.

The beginning was exquisitely painful, as the woman at the well resisted Him. But the end was remarkable. Exposed, convicted, humbled, deconstructed, ready to be renewed, she turned to Christ. She quit her old manner of life and was filled with Jesus.

It is a privilege beyond price to witness such a work of divine grace, when every excuse is silenced, hardened ground is plowed up in felt conviction, and the grace of Jesus becomes the most desirable gift in the world. Then the Word of Christ in Scripture is devoured and the lips instinctively speak of Him—that is the beginning of revival. It is glorious. The pain of it, as countless narratives of revival conversion underline, is at times overwhelming, almost physically unbearable. But its cleansing impact can be breathtaking in its staggering directness and simplicity.

In view of this, there is a question we need to ask about our own church fellowships and about ourselves. Are we living in an unrevived condition? If the honest answer shocks, let it also draw from us an honest prayer for Christ to do a new work in our lives.

But a further question must be faced. I may be enthusiastic about the harvest, but am I willing for the plow to cut into me, disturb my weed-infested heart, show me my as-yet-unimagined need, and lead me to see Christ as sin-bearer and Savior in ways that will demand my all?

That is exactly what "Love so amazing, so divine"[22] demands—nothing less than everything.

# 21

# ONE NIGHT ONLY

Saturday morning break time arrived during the conference at which I was a guest, and it seemed a good idea to take a stroll outside. It had been dark the night before, and the church building across the road had been only a dark shadow. Now, as I walked over to have a look, I was startled by the words on the notice board: "Revival Here Next Week: Tuesday, Thursday, and Friday." So it is true, I thought. There really are Christians who believe that a church can plan, prepare for, and announce revival in advance!

It would have been easy to be cynical and clever (Why no revival on Wednesday?) or lofty and superior (Don't these people know how mistaken Charles Finney was?). Probably the folks across the road were simply planning a Bible conference like the one at which I was speaking—a time of more intensive ministry that would refresh and even "revive" them. Surely, I mused, no one who has experienced revival in the historic sense would advertise the dates on which it would take place. True revival has a very different effect.

But what is the difference?

## *The Distinguishing Marks*

Young bank tellers used to be taught to distinguish forged bank notes from real ones by spending hours handling the genuine article. By the same token, the best safeguard against mistaken revival*ism* is familiarity with the real thing—revival.

In his *Distinguishing Marks of a Work of the Spirit of God*, Jonathan Edwards draws on 1 John 4 to show that all true works of God share several features:

1. A high esteem for Christ.
2. The overthrow of Satan's kingdom in our hearts.
3. A reverent view of, and close attention to, God's Word in Scripture.
4. The presence of the Spirit of truth convincing us of the reality of eternity and the depth of our sin and need.
5. A deep love for both God and man.

But what does this mean in real-life terms?

## A Microcosmic View

Many years ago, I witnessed revival in its most microcosmic form in a sudden, unexpected, and remarkable work of God's Spirit on a friend. The work was so dramatic, the effect so radical, that news of it spread quickly to different parts of the country. People were asking, "Just what exactly happened?"

It was twenty-five years before I felt it appropriate to ask my friend (who, at the time, had certainly been unfamiliar with Edwards' *Distinguishing Marks*) what this remarkable experience had involved. The answer was illuminating. Five things seemed to have happened, and they were still fresh in the memory two and a half decades later:

1. *A painful exposure of the particular sin of unbelief occurred.* Listening to preaching was a staple of my friend's spiritual diet, but what came with overpowering force was a sense that God's Word had actually been despised inwardly. God's own Word, preached in the power of the Spirit, stripped away the mask of inner pride and outward reputation for spirituality. There was a fearful exposure of sin.

2. *A powerful desire arose to be free from all sin.* A new affection came, as if unbidden, into the heart. Indeed, a desire seemed to be given actually to have sin increasingly revealed and exposed in order that it might be confessed, pardoned, and cleansed. Disturbing though it was, there was a sweetness of grace in the pain.

3. *The love of Christ now seemed marvelous beyond measure.* A love for Him flowed from a heart that could not get enough of Christ, ransacking Scripture to discover more and more about Him.

4. *A new love for God's Word was born*—for reading it, for hearing it expounded and applied, and especially for knowing every expression of God's will, *so that it might be obeyed.*

5. *A compassionate love for others now flowed.* It came from this double sense of sin and need on the one hand and grace and forgiveness on the other. Christian witness ceased to be a burden and became the expression of Spirit-wrought and powerful new affections.

It was thus for King David:

*Have mercy upon me, O God . . . according to the multitude of Your tender mercies, blot out my transgressions. Wash me thoroughly from my iniquity, and cleanse me from my sin. For I acknowledge my transgressions, and my sin is always before me. Against You, You only, have I sinned, and done this evil in Your sight. . . . Purge me . . . wash me. . . . Create in me a clean heart, O God. . . . My tongue shall sing aloud of Your righteousness.*

—PSALM 51:1–4, 7, 10, 14

There are echoes of this in Jonah, the prophet who needed personal revival before he became God's instrument for Ninevite revival: "I cried out to the LORD. . . . I said, 'I have been cast out of Your sight.' . . . You have brought up my life. . . . I will sacrifice to You with the voice of thanksgiving" (Jonah 2:1–9).

## Preserved from Two Dangers

When the Spirit comes, He convicts of sin, righteousness, and judgment (John 16:8–11). His work is the real thing. It preserves us from two dangers. The first is the (Arminian) danger of false revivalism. Familiarity with the genuine is the best safeguard against the false. The second is the (Reformed?) danger of a false superiority. Accurate knowledge about the nature of revival is not the same thing as being revived! Here, as elsewhere, Paul's wise teaching needs to be taken to heart: knowledge can puff up; love builds up (1 Cor. 13). For of what value is it before God to be capable of exposing the false if we have no desire ourselves for the true?

At the end of the day, the best safeguard against false revivalism is experiential knowledge of the true. Ultimately, that is less a desire for revival than it is a desire for the knowledge of God.

# 22

# JOY THROUGH LIGHT

The Reformers placed tremendous stress on the gifts of the Holy Spirit to the whole body of Christ. B. B. Warfield rightly described John Calvin as "the theologian of the Holy Spirit."[23] Yet Reformed Christians have always received "bad press" for their views on the gifts of the Spirit.

Paradoxically, however, the source of the "bad press" has changed during the past five hundred years. In the sixteenth century, it was Roman Catholicism ("Where are the miracles to authenticate your message?" Rome asked). Yesterday, it was Pentecostalism. Today, however, it seems to be evangelicalism as a whole. It is now regarded as reactionary, even denigratory to the Holy Spirit, to hold the view that certain gifts, such as prophecy, miracle working, and tongues, were intended to function specifically during the apostolic age and not to continue at every time of the church's history.

It ought to be beyond dispute that God can do whatever pleases Him. We can trust Him to do that because He is holy, wise, almighty, and wonderfully good and kind. Yet, at the same time, we are called to search the Scriptures to learn what He specifically has promised to do, since this is what faith rests in and expects Him to do.

In this context, Scripture teaches us that God purposefully gave some gifts (specifically the gift of revelatory prophecy, the ability to work miracles, and tongues) for limited periods of time and with specific ends in view.

There are solid biblical reasons for believing this:

1. It is characteristic of the pattern of God's working throughout all biblical history.

Contrary to popular opinion, "miraculous" gifts actually were given only spasmodically in biblical history. Their occurrence is generally contained within a handful of time periods lasting around a generation each. The statement that the Bible is a book "full of the miraculous" needs to be carefully nuanced or it easily becomes misleading.

2. The function of these gifts—namely, to convey and to confirm new revelation (now ceased until Christ's return)—is underlined several times in the New Testament (Acts 2:22; 14:3; cf. 2 Cor. 12:12; Heb. 2:3–4).

3. The text of the New Testament suggests that by the close of the apostolic age the role of these gifts was already being superseded by the apostolic writings. Thus, for example, there is no reference to their *presence* or to their *future regulation* in the Pastoral Letters (1, 2 Timothy and Titus), among the last epistles written.

### Analogies?

More could be said here in terms of biblical Christology. The outpouring of the gifts of prophecy, miracles, and tongues at Pentecost was specifically intended to mark the coronation of Christ. These gifts, therefore, were inherently intended to be non-permanent features of the life of the church.

But in this context it is probably just as important, if not more so, to emphasize another, often-ignored facet of Reformed teaching. It is well expressed in some words of the great Puritan John Owen:

> Although all these gifts and operations ceased in some respect, some of them absolutely, and some of them as to the immediate manner of communication and degree of excellency; yet so far as the edification of the church was concerned in them, something that is analogous unto them was and is continued.[24]

What does this mean? Simply this: the same Spirit gives both temporary and continuing gifts to the church. We should not be surprised, therefore, to discover common threads running through both.

Perhaps the most important common thread is the Spirit's ministry in illumination—He enlightens our minds to enable us to know, see, grasp, and apply the will and purposes of God. There was an immediacy to illumination in the temporary gifts God gave. The Spirit taught the apostles "all things" (John 14:26) and led them into all truth (John 16:13). Now, however, He continues this work in us through the Scriptures He enabled the apostles to write for us.

Indeed, in the upper room (John 13–17), our Lord made it clear to the apostles that this would be one of the central ministries of the Spirit in their lives. He would remind them of what Jesus had said (Gospels), lead them into the truth (Epistles), and show them the things to come (Revelation). He does a similar work in our lives. But while He illuminated the minds of the apostles in relationship to His action in history, He illumines our minds in relation to their words in Scripture.

## The Thirst for the Immediate

Why, then, should Christians today—by contrast with their fathers—be so thirsty to experience immediate personal revelation from God ("God told me . . .") when His desire for us is the ongoing work of the Spirit opening up our understanding through the mediated revelation of the New Testament?

There seem to be three reasons:

1. It may appear to be more exciting, more obviously supernatural, to have direct revelation rather than Bible revelation. It seems to many people to be more "spiritual," more "divine," more "personal."

2. To many people, it feels much more convincing to be able to say, "God has told me . . ." than to say, "The Bible tells me. . . ."

3. Direct revelation makes it unnecessary to engage in painstaking Bible study and careful consideration of Christian doctrine in order to know the will of God. By comparison with immediate revelation, Bible study seems—to be frank—boring. Although rarely said, underlying all of this is a sinister thought: the Bible is not very clear. By contrast, it is assumed that direct revelation cannot possibly be misunderstood.

## *Unveiling Illumination*

Lest we be browbeaten and develop a kind of siege mentality in response to this, here are some things we should bear in mind about this work of illumination:

1. This was actually Jesus' experience. Yes, our Lord prophesied; yes, He worked miracles. But to ignore the fact that He studied and memorized the Scriptures, then applied them to Himself, would make us guilty of Docetism (the view that Jesus' humanity only seemed to be like ours). Jesus grew in wisdom and favor with God (Luke 2:52) by patiently meditating on the Old Testament Scriptures. (I suspect He probably knew them by heart.)

Isaiah's third Servant Song gives us an extraordinarily moving picture of the Lord Jesus waking up each day, dependent on His Father to illumine His understanding of His Word to enable Him to think, feel, act, and live as the Man full of the Spirit of wisdom and understanding (cf. Isa. 11:2ff):

> *The Lord GOD has given Me*
> *The tongue of the learned,*
> *That I should know how to speak*
> *A word in season to him who is weary.*
> *He awakens Me morning by morning,*
> *He awakens My ear*
> *To hear as the learned.*
>
> —ISAIAH 50:4

2. This is the divine method that produces authentic Christian growth, because it involves the renewal of the mind (Rom. 12:2) and it is progressive (it takes time and demands the obedience of our wills). Sometimes God does things quickly. But His ordinary way with His children is to work slowly and surely to make us progressively more like our Lord Jesus. Trees do not grow overnight; they grow over long periods of time, and experience sun, rain, and wind to help them in the process. So it is with the trees of the Lord's planting. Here the watchword is found in Paul's counsel to Timothy:

"Think over what I say, for the Lord will give you understanding . . ." (2 Tim. 2:7, ESV).

3. The result of the Spirit working with and through the Word of God to illumine and transform our thinking is the development of a godly instinct that operates in sometimes surprising ways. In a well-taught, Spirit-illumined believer, the revelation of Scripture becomes so much a part of his or her mindset that the will of God frequently seems to become clear instinctively, and in that sense "immediately." Just as a well-trained and experienced musical ear recognizes whether a piece of music is played well or badly, so spiritual exercise in the Word of God creates discernment (see Heb. 5:11–14).

This may help to explain why well-meaning Christians have sometimes mistaken illumination for revelation. Confusing the labels sometimes can lead to potentially unhappy practical consequences.

In addition, understanding that these are the Lord's ways with us helps to explain some of the more mysterious elements in our experience without forcing us to resort to the claim that we have the gift of special revelation or prophecy. Here the late Professor John Murray spoke with great wisdom:

> As we are the subjects of this illumination and are responsive to it, and as the Holy Spirit is operative in us to the doing of God's will, we shall have feelings, impressions, convictions, urges, inhibitions, impulses, burdens, resolutions. Illumination and direction by the Spirit through the Word of God will focus themselves in our consciousness in these ways. We are not automata. . . . We must not think [these things] are . . . necessarily irrational or fanatically mystical.[25]

God's Word, illumined by God's Spirit, as Psalm 119 so magnificently shows, is the pathway to spiritual stability and liberty. It leads us unwaveringly to knowing, loving, and doing God's will on a daily basis.

Yes, there is joy through light.

# PART IV

# The Privileges of Grace

*Christians in a past day sometimes spoke about "living below the level of our privileges." Growing stronger in living for Christ depends on understanding and entering into all of the privileges that are ours in Christ.*

# 23

# Our Union with Christ

In His Farewell Discourse, in addition to clearly revealing God as Father, Son, and Holy Spirit, our Lord wonderfully unfolds the central theme of the union that exists between Himself and His people, and the blessings that flow from it. He describes this union to His disciples in startling words: "You are in me, and I am in you" (John 14:20, NIV); to His Father, He expresses it even more simply: "I in them" (John 17:23).

So profound and important is this truth that Jesus provides two analogies to help us follow His teaching, one heavenly and the other earthly.

## Two Analogies

The first analogy helps us to grasp the sheer wonder of our union with Christ: "At that day [the Day of Pentecost, when the Spirit came] you will know that I am in My Father, and you in Me, and I in you" (John 14:20). The foundation for and analogy of the believer's union with Christ is His own union with His Father. So intimate is our relation with the Savior.

The second analogy helps us to grasp its nature: we are united to Christ as branches are united to a vine. Jesus is the Vine, we are the branches. This analogy is developed at length in John 15:1–11.

These words take us to the next stage in the series of "I am" sayings in John's Gospel. In these sayings, Jesus is set before us as the fulfillment of events and patterns in the history of redemption.

Frequently in the Old Testament, Israel is described as a vine (Ps. 80:8–16;

Isa. 5:1–7; Ezek. 19:10–14). Interestingly, this picture language is used in the context of judgment, for while Israel was planted by God, she failed to bear proper fruit. By contrast, Jesus is the true fruit-bearing vine planted by the Gardener, the Father. His desire is to see us—cuttings grafted by grace into the vine—remain, abide, or, as gardeners say, "take" (John 15:4–7), and bear fruit. But what does this involve?

## Abiding in Christ

The exhortation to "abide" has been frequently misunderstood, as though it were a special, mystical, and indefinable experience. But Jesus makes clear that it actually involves a number of concrete realities.

First, union with our Lord depends on His grace. Of course we are actively and personally united to Christ by faith (John 14:12). But faith itself is rooted in the activity of God. It is the Father who, as the divine Gardener, has grafted us into Christ. It is Christ, by His Word, who has cleansed us to fit us for union with Himself (15:3). All is sovereign, all is of grace.

Second, union with Christ means being obedient to Him. Abiding involves our response to the teaching of Jesus: "If you abide in Me, and My words abide in you . . ." (John 15:7a). Paul echoes this idea in Colossians 3:16, where he writes, "Let the word of Christ dwell in you richly," a statement closely related to his parallel exhortation in Ephesians 5:18: "be filled with the Spirit."

In a nutshell, abiding in Christ means allowing His Word to fill our minds, direct our wills, and transform our affections. In other words, our relationship to Christ is intimately connected to what we do with our Bibles! Then, of course, as Christ's Word dwells in us and the Spirit fills us, we will begin to pray in a way consistent with the will of God and discover the truth of our Lord's often misapplied promise: "You will ask what you desire, and it shall be done for you" (John 15:7b).

Third, Christ underlines a further principle, "Abide in My love" (15:9), and states very clearly what this implies: the believer rests his or her life on the love of Christ (the love of the One who lays down His life for His friends, v. 13).

This love has been proved to us in the cross of Christ. We must never allow ourselves to drift from daily contemplation of the cross as the irrefutable demonstration of that love, or from dependence on the Spirit who sheds it abroad in our hearts (Rom. 5:5). Furthermore, remaining in Christ's love comes to very concrete expression: simple obedience rendered to Him is the fruit and evidence of love for Him (John 15:10–14).

## The Pruning Knife

Finally, we are called, as part of the abiding process, to submit to the pruning knife of God in the providences by which He cuts away all disloyalty and sometimes all that is unimportant, in order that we might remain in Christ all the more wholeheartedly.

In the horticultural world, pruning generally is done with a view to long-term fruitfulness. So with believers—the Father prunes the branches of the true vine in order that they may yield more fruit. Of course, there often seems to be an apparent randomness in His cutting, but there is never a wasted stroke—every cut is necessary for us to "bear more fruit" (John 15:2). In Christ, we are safe under the Father's pruning knife.

If we need any more encouragement to remain in Christ, we can find it in the reason Jesus gives for this teaching: "These things I have spoken to you, that My joy may remain in you, and that your joy may be full" (John 15:11).

Did Jesus mean that He said these things so that His disciples—and we with them—might receive joy from Him? Or did He mean that we will give Him joy?

Both, surely! For not only are we united to Him—He has determined that His joy and ours are now inseparable!

# 24

# THE INDWELLING
# CHRIST

The great Christmas and Easter hymns capture aspects of biblical teaching that we sometimes tend to overlook. They brilliantly celebrate the truth that the historical events of the gospel have profound personal implications for us.

At Easter time, we are reminded that as Christ died and rose, so in Him we have died to the powers that held us in bondage and have been raised into new life. "*Ours* the cross, the grave, the skies," as Charles Wesley puts it.[26]

The same is true of the great Christmas carols. While they rightly emphasize that Jesus is Immanuel, God come to dwell *with* us, they also underline that He is Christ, the incarnate One, come to dwell *in* us. So the rough and sometimes harsh-tongued Reformer Martin Luther sweetly teaches us to sing:

*Ah! dearest Jesus, Holy Child,*
*Make Thee a bed, soft, undefiled,*
*Within my heart, that it may be*
*A quiet chamber kept for Thee.*[27]

The wonder of the Christmas message here celebrated is that, through faith, Jesus Christ comes to indwell His people. His presence is not merely an event in history but the experience of every Christian believer. Our understanding of the Christmas message and its life-changing implications will be incomplete unless this truth dawns upon us.

The New Testament tends to stress our life in Christ rather than His life in us. But there are perhaps a dozen major passages in the New Testament that emphasize Christ's indwelling. Their teaching raises two questions. First, in what way does Christ indwell us? Second, what difference does it make to our lives?

## Christ Indwells

How does Christ indwell us?

The Son of God came to dwell in human flesh *for us* in order that He might come to dwell *in us* by His Spirit. This is the meaning of Jesus' teaching prior to His death: "Remain in me, and I will remain in you" (John 15:4, NIV). He goes on to say that this is the way to bear much fruit.

Later, in prayer, Jesus spoke again of this union in these terms: "I in them and you in me. . . . I have made you known to them . . . in order that . . . I myself may be in them" (John 17:23, 26, NIV). Just as the Father "dwells" in the Son (and vice versa), so the Son dwells in believers (and vice versa). The indwelling of Christ in His people is so significant that its best analogy is the mutual indwelling of the Father and the Son.

Jesus had already indicated to the disciples that His indwelling would be through the indwelling of the Holy Spirit. The Spirit would come as "another Helper" (John 14:16). The nuance of John's language here is that the Spirit is "another just like Jesus," for the promise of the coming of the Spirit to indwell the disciples is parallel to Jesus' other promise: "I will not leave you orphans; I will come to you" (John 14:18). Jesus added that when this would take place (on the Day of Pentecost), the disciples would "know that . . . you [are] in Me, and I in you" (John 14:20).

Paul expresses the same perspective when he speaks about the indwelling of Christ in Romans 8:9–11. Several statements are parallel to and mutually explain one another: "The Spirit of God dwells in you" (v. 9); "Christ is in you" (v. 10); "the Spirit of Him who raised Jesus from the dead [i.e., the Father] dwells in you . . . His Spirit who dwells in you" (v. 11).

For Paul, to have Christ is to have the Spirit, because Christ indwells us through the Spirit.

Does the indwelling of the Spirit seem a poor substitute for Jesus Himself? Not when we remember the identity of this Spirit. He is the One who was present at the conception of Jesus (Luke 1:35) and who enabled Him to grow in wisdom and grace (Luke 2:40, 52; cf. the Messianic promise in Isaiah 11:1–3). He is the Spirit who came upon Jesus at His baptism and served as the strategist of His campaign against the powers of darkness (Luke 3:22; 4:1). Through the Spirit, Christ offered Himself on the cross (Heb. 9:14), and by His power Jesus was raised from the dead (Rom. 1:4).

To be indwelt by the Spirit, therefore, is to have communion with Christ incarnate, obedient, crucified, resurrected, and glorified. "By this we know that He abides in us, by the Spirit whom He has given us" (1 John 3:24). No wonder Henry F. Lyte, the hymn writer, bids us, "Think what Spirit dwells within thee."[28]

### The Difference

What difference does it make that Christ indwells us? There are several effects:

1. The fact that Christ has come to indwell us changes the fundamental direction of our lives, according to the New Testament. "It is no longer I who live," says Paul, "but Christ lives in me" (Gal. 2:20). The old life, dominated by sin, Satan, and self, has gone. Christ has come to take possession of our whole beings and to provide all the resources we need to live for Him. Life is no longer a matter of frustrated striving to keep an external code, but it is living in the power of the indwelling Christ. His yoke fits well; the burden of His royal law is light because He has come to shoulder it from within, in the power of the Spirit (cf. Rom. 8:3–4).

2. Yet immediately when Christ indwells an individual, his or her life becomes a spiritual battlefield. Think of two statements Paul makes, employing similar language: "It is no longer I who live, but Christ lives in

me" (Gal. 2:20) and "It is no longer I who do it, but sin that dwells in me" (Rom. 7:17).

Here is a mysterious paradox. Christ dwells in Paul, yet sin also continues to dwell in him. Conflict is unavoidable; opposition to Christ's influence is as inevitable as the hostility of King Herod to the Christ child when he feared that the newborn babe was a threat to his throne (Matt. 2:16; cf. Rev. 12:1–6). However, though the conflict is certainly between opposite foes, they are not equal. The One who is in us is greater than all opposition (cf. 1 John 4:4). If Christ indwells us, we need no longer be defeated by sin.

3. Our attitude and response to every fellow Christian must be consciously dominated by the thought that he or she is indwelt by the same Christ who indwells us. This is a simple, logical deduction from the fact that Christ has come to indwell us—but its potential repercussions are staggering.

Other Christians are temples of Christ by the Spirit; they are saints, holy ones set apart for the Lord. Consequently, no natural distinction between us and fellow believers (race, color, education, employment, wealth) can be allowed to become a barrier between us, for "Christ is all and in all" (Col. 3:11). How different our relationships, our thoughts, our speech, and our actions would be among the saints if we were more conscious of that!

4. If Christ indwells us by His Spirit so that we are united to Him— married to Him, as it were—then our very bodies are His (1 Cor. 6:12–17). Our eyes and what we see, our lips and what we say, our hands and what we touch, our feet and where we go—all are His. Do you live in the conscious awareness of that, yielding your body to Him because He has redeemed it and now wants to sanctify it?

The message of the incarnate Christ is glorious indeed, but it must never be severed from the message of the indwelling Christ. He who came for us as a baby now dwells in us as the Lord of glory through His Spirit. That is His gift to us.

The indwelling Christ seeks one gift from you in return.

You.

# 25

# SHARING CHRIST'S INHERITANCE

I n the opening chapter of Ephesians, Paul provides the broadest possible perspective on what it means to be a Christian. He traces the origins of our salvation back to the choice of God in eternity past (Eph. 1:4) and looks forward to its consummation in the glories of eternity to come (Eph. 1:10).

The overpowering nature of this vision sometimes makes us lose sight of one particular feature of Paul's teaching that is of immense importance to him: his exposition is saturated in family language. The *Father* chose us (v. 3) to be *adopted as His sons* (v. 5). He has given us His Spirit as the guarantee of our *inheritance* (v. 14). He prays to the *Father of glory* (v. 17) that our eyes may be opened to appreciate *His glorious inheritance* in the saints (v. 18).

Salvation means being brought into the privileges of life in a new family. If you are an adopted child of God, you are *an heir of God and a co-heir with Christ* (Rom. 8:17). You are rich.

## *The Heir*

To become an heir means to receive the right to possess riches first possessed by another. The idea has a special significance in biblical teaching. The Father is the Creator and Lord of all. But in His generous love, the wealth of the universe was to be the inheritance of Adam as God's image and son (Gen. 1:26; Luke 3:38). When Adam was but a "child," God gave him part of his inheritance, the Garden of Eden, to take responsibility for and to enjoy.

But Adam tried to steal what was not his; as a result, he forfeited his entire inheritance through his sin. Esau-like, Adam and Eve sold Eden for "a mess of pottage" and were barred from the garden that had been the firstfruits of their inheritance.

But the Father was determined that the inheritance should be restored. Indeed, He already had drawn up plans for its restoration. He gave advance intimation of it: the Seed of Eve would crush the head of the serpent whose temptations had led to the catastrophe (Gen. 3:15). Abraham, too, was later made familiar with the plan. In his seed all the nations would inherit blessing rather than cursing (Gen. 12:3).

Slowly, an outline of the strategy became visible through divine revelation: the Seed of the woman, a descendant of Abraham, a son of David, a messianic Prophet, Priest, and King, and a Suffering Servant—one Man who was also the Son of God—would fulfill all the promises of God. He would be a second Man, making a new beginning. He would also be the last Adam. He would do all that Adam had failed to accomplish in order to enter into a full inheritance. But He would forfeit His own life in order to bear the divine punishment for Adamic sin. He, unlike Adam, would be meek and inherit the earth. In Him the right of inheritance would be restored. He would be "appointed heir of all things" (Heb. 1:2).

Sure enough, the Heir came. He obeyed the Father and resisted temptation where Adam had yielded. By His obedience He gained the right to possess the entire inheritance. Now everything belongs to Christ. He is "the firstborn over all creation" (Col. 1:15); all authority in heaven and earth is His, including power over sin, death, and Satan (Matt. 28:18); in Him are hidden all the treasures of wisdom and knowledge, for in Him is the fullness of God (Col. 2:3; 1:19).

This Son and Heir heard His Father say, "Ask of Me, and I will give You the nations for Your inheritance" (Ps. 2:8). But the Son replied, "Father, let Me share My inheritance with the poor and the disinherited. Adopt them into Your family as Your sons, too; give them My Spirit [see Acts 2:33; Rom. 8:15]; let them use My name [see John 16:24]."

The Father heard the prayer of the Son; He made us His children.

Listen, then, to Paul's reasoning: now, if we are children, we are heirs (Rom. 8:17).

## Our Inheritance

According to the Law, as Paul knew, the firstborn son received a double inheritance, while all the others received a single portion (Deut. 21:17; cf. 2 Kings 2:9). But neither the Father nor the Son binds Himself to the limits of the Law. Paul declares: "[We are all] heirs of God and joint heirs with Christ" (Rom. 8:17).

Do you see the implication? *All* that belongs to the last Adam is for us. As the early church fathers delighted in saying, Christ took what was ours so that we might receive what was His. All that is His is ours: "All things are yours: . . . the world or life or death, or things present or things to come—all are yours. And you are Christ's, and Christ is God's" (1 Cor. 3:21–23).

When I was a boy in Scotland, I occasionally read puzzling notices in the local newspaper, such as the following:

Will Angus MacDonald please contact McKay, Campbell, and Ross (Solicitors) at 10 Bannockburn Street, where he will learn something to his advantage.

I did not realize then what those cryptic words, "something to his advantage," meant. Angus, whoever he was, was a beneficiary of someone's will, and he did not yet know it. Angus had suddenly become a rich man.

But what if Angus did not see and respond to the notice? Then his poverty continued. If Angus did not pursue his claim to his inheritance, he did not taste its riches.

Do not make that mistake! If you are a Christian, then you are rich in Christ; enjoy and share your riches.

# 26

# BORN AGAIN—BUT
# ONLY FROM ABOVE

G od will not give His glory to another (Isa. 42:8). Therefore, the triune Lord begins and extends His work in a style that underscores His glory alone.

In the Bible, this pattern becomes a kind of leitmotif. For instance, God's sovereign action in Creation serves as a model for His equally sovereign action in our spiritual re-creation. Paul never ceases to be amazed that the same God who said, "'Let light shine out of darkness,' made his light shine in our hearts to give us the light of the knowledge of the glory of God in the face of Christ" (2 Cor. 4:6, NIV). Of this new creation in Christ, he says, "All this is from God" (2 Cor. 5:18, NIV). This is not creation out of nothing, but a new creation out of the twisted, distorted condition into which we had fallen.

Similarly, God in His sovereignty gives new life where there is barrenness. God's covenant with Abraham and Sarah is an example. It is in this way that the true seed of Abraham is conceived. Later, the Lord came to Manoah and his wife, "who was sterile" (Judg. 13:2, NIV), and Samson was born. Then He came to Hannah, the barren wife of Elkanah, and Samuel was born (1 Sam. 1:1–20). Later yet, he came to the elderly Zacharias and the barren Elizabeth, and John the Baptist was born (Luke 1:5ff).

But all this merely paved the way for the greatest example: the Spirit overshadowed Mary, a virgin, and the Head of God's new creation was conceived and later born. In His sovereignty, God makes the barren womb bear new life.

This is the pattern of divine sovereignty that lies behind Jesus' words to Nicodemus: "You must be born again [or, from above]" (John 3:7). God alone can give new life where there is barrenness and emptiness.

Like so many others before and after him, poor Nicodemus could not understand what Jesus meant. He expected Jesus to tell him what he must do to participate in this new work of God (John 3:2). But what could he possibly do? Could he return to his mother's womb and be born "a second time" (John 3:4)? Although he was a (perhaps *the*) great theologian in Israel (John 3:10), he had not understood the teaching of the Old Testament that emphasized the sovereignty of God in giving new life (see Jer. 31:33; Ezek. 36:25–27). That life begins with God's working, not with our "doing."

Our Lord patiently explained why birth from above is so necessary.

## We Are Flesh

Flesh gives birth to flesh; only the Spirit can give birth to spirit (John 3:6).

Ask the man who is in the flesh to engage in truly spiritual exercises, and he eventually collapses in exhaustion or despair. Reading Scripture, singing praises, spending time in prayer, giving ready obedience to the commandments—these are burdens that break him, not (as they become for the regenerate) wings that enable him to fly.

## We Are Spiritually Blind

Jesus taught that without new birth, we cannot see the kingdom of God (John 3:3). Unless we have been born from above, we simply cannot detect spiritual realities when they are placed before us.

Nicodemus could not see Jesus' point. Brilliant man though he presumably was, he could not make the connection between Jesus' teaching on the necessity of a new birth and his own spiritual powerlessness.

Spiritual understanding is not achieved by means of natural intelligence or by academic learning. "The natural man does not receive the things of the Spirit of God, for they are foolishness to him; nor can he know them, because they are spiritually discerned" (1 Cor. 2:14).

## We Are in Bondage

Without new birth, we cannot enter the kingdom of God (John 3:5). Try as we might, we are in chains.

Later, Jesus would teach that those who commit sin are slaves of sin (John 8:34). There are no resources in us by nature from which new and holy life can spring. We are barren and bankrupt. Spiritual life, therefore, must come "not of natural descent, nor of human decision or a husband's will, but . . . of God" (John 1:13, NIV).

Is there a clearer example that a man can be religious, sincere, thoroughly decent, theologically well-educated, and yet blind, helpless, and spiritually barren? Nicodemus illustrates well why our Lord insists that the new birth must be seen as a sovereign and divine work. It is not simply because it fits in well with the Calvinistic scheme of things. No, it is because, as the *Book of Common Prayer* (1662) says, "there is no health in us."

I have very occasionally heard people sing about having free will to accept the gospel, but never of anyone praying, and far less singing, that God would simply leave the unconverted to their own free will in spiritual matters. No, we cry to God to arrest them, regenerate them, and save them. With energy and feeling we sing with Augustus M. Toplady, "Thou must save, and thou alone."[29] Those are instincts fashioned from reading Scripture. The new birth is God's work. It is so by necessity, for we are helpless and empty.

A lady once asked George Whitefield why he so often insisted on preaching on these words: "You must be born again." Whitefield replied, "Because, Madam, you must." The simple truth is that there is no other way into the kingdom. The only way in is by the one thing we need and can never do for ourselves: new birth. God alone can do it.

If we fail to see the depth of our need here, divine sovereignty inevitably will taste bitter to us, for it challenges our self-sufficiency and our easy assumption that we can contribute to our salvation. Become aware of our sinful condition, however, and divine sovereignty becomes sweeter than honey, for it teaches us not only that God alone can regenerate us but also that He graciously does so. Like everything else in the Christian life, the way up is down—down with pride and self-sufficiency—and then up by grace to glory.

"But," someone is bound to say, "this teaching would drive people to despair of themselves." But of course! That is the forerunner to being drawn away from our own resources to seek and find salvation in Christ. But then, as the Spirit works, we discover that the new birth He gives does not take place over our heads but in our lives. We believe in Christ; we are cleansed, renewed, changed; we see and enter the kingdom—we become new men and women in Christ.

Yes, of course there is more. But there is never less. Neither is there any other foundation for new life than this: God chose to give us birth, and He has done so.

Well, why else would you cast yourself on the mercy of God?

# 27

# New Wine for Old

John's Gospel was written to bring us to faith in the Son of God (John 20:31). His portrayal of Jesus involves the creation of a tapestry of events and discourses. To weave the tapestry panels, he used various threads drawn from the Old Testament.

One of these panels is in John 2:1–4:54. That this is a distinct section in the Gospel tapestry is indicated by the fact that both its beginning and ending are located in Cana (2:1; 4:46). Running through these three chapters is one particular thread that helps us to trace the meaning of the gospel more easily: Jesus fulfills and supersedes the old Mosaic order.

## New Wine

As a guest at a wedding in Cana, Jesus changed into wine the water that the Jews used for ceremonial washing (2:6). He turned a situation in which resources had run out into a foretaste of the great wedding banquet of the messianic age.

What was Jesus doing? On the one hand, He was showing the inadequacy of the provisions of the old order. The sacrificial system could not bring the joy He offered. The old water gave only ceremonial forgiveness, and therefore short-lived and fading joy. But on the other hand, the Lord was demonstrating that in the gospel there is new wine that offers lasting joy (Isa. 55:1–3). Jesus Himself gives that wine.

## New Temple

Later in John 2, Jesus cleansed the temple. Presumably there was anger in the voices that demanded to know His credentials. On what authority did He do this? He answered by a prophetic appeal to His own death and resurrection couched in terms of the destruction and raising again of another temple (2:19–22).

Could any more daring way have been found to express the old order's inadequacy? To a Jew, the temple was the most important building on earth. To Jesus, however, it was but a shadow, a temporary context for entering the presence of God. Christ was the reality to which such shadows pointed. He was God the Son come to "tabernacle among us" (John 1:14). Jesus Himself is the new temple.

## New Birth

The famous conversation with Nicodemus continued the theme. Although he sought out Jesus under cover of darkness (John 3:2), he nevertheless represented the highest and the best of the old order, being a member of the Sanhedrin (v. 1) and Israel's theologian (v. 10). Yet he did not understand what was implicit in the revelation God had given in the Scriptures.

Only the dawning of the new age of the Messiah could meet the needs of sinners for cleansing and renewal. But Nicodemus should have known this already from his Old Testament studies (Ezek. 36:25–27). Nothing less than the life that comes down from above could bring Nicodemus (and all who are like him) into the kingdom. All his learning could not accomplish that. Only new birth can bring one into the kingdom of God (John 3:3, 5). Jesus Himself gives that new birth.

## New Water

This same richly colored thread is woven into the wonderful narrative of our Lord's conversation with the Samaritan woman who came to draw water from Jacob's Well. In describing their meeting, John stressed a detail that at first sight seems to add little to the actual story: they met in what was Jacob's territory (John 4:5–6). This information is included to highlight the point of contact between Jesus and this anonymous water bearer. The woman put her finger on the issue when she seemed to ridicule our Lord's offer of water: "Are You greater than our father Jacob . . . ?" (v. 12).

That was precisely the point: He was indeed greater, much greater! The patriarchs were merely the ones to whom the promise was given; Jesus was the fulfillment of the promise, the Messiah who was to come (vv. 25–26). Jacob's water would eventually leave the woman thirsty; now she was offered water that could satisfy her thirst permanently (vv. 13–14). Jesus Himself pours out this new water (7:37–39).

## New Life

The fascinating little story that concludes this section, and leads on to the next, records the plight of a royal official (John 4:46–54). He was employed by Herod the Tetrarch. His son lay dying.

This man already had two "strikes" against him—a harsh master and a dying son. Some scholars have surmised a third—he may well have been a Gentile. His case was hopeless; there was nothing he could do to give life to his son. Neither could the Law of Moses do that for him. It could only tell his son how to live, condemn him for any failure, and—in the broadest sense—point forward to the One who could help. What was wanted and needed was new life. Jesus Himself gives this new life.

What are we meant to see in these various incidents that make up this panel in the tapestry of John's theology? His comment in John 2:11 gives us the clue to the whole: Jesus "revealed his glory, and his disciples put their faith in him" (NIV).

John had already explained this principle in 1:17. The law, the commands, and the shadowy reflections of salvation came through Moses. But the law did not possess within itself the reality to which it pointed. That reality—grace and truth in substance—came only through Christ.

What, then, does this spiritual tapestry panel display? Among other things, it presents a series of probing questions:

Are you enjoying the new gospel wine?

Do you worship in the new temple and display the marks of the new birth? Have you found satisfaction in the new water?

Do you enjoy new life as someone who has been raised from spiritual death into life and clothed in garments of salvation?

Well?

# 28

# SALVATION IN
# THREE TENSES

*Time present and time past*
*Are both perhaps present in time future,*
*And time future contained in time past.*[30]

T. S. Eliot's rhythmic words above, from the poem "Burnt Norton,"
simply and eloquently describe the ordinary flow of history. But
the letter to the Hebrews presents a very different perspective on
God's purposes and patterns in that flow. From the perspective of the author
of Hebrews, it would be true to say that the future determines the past and
the present rather than the other way around. In other words, to understand
Hebrews—and thus to understand how the Bible as a whole works—we
need to understand a riddle:

*The invisible is more substantial than the visible;*
*The future shapes the past;*
*The new is more fundamental than the old.*

What does all this mean?

Simply put, it means that the story of the Lord Jesus, His person and work,
is not a divine afterthought, a heavenly plan B hurriedly scrambled together
when plan A went horribly wrong in Eden. No, the coming of Christ was

in the plan before the fall. Everything that precedes it chronologically actually follows it logically.

From one point of view, of course, the Old Testament served as the model of what Christ would come to accomplish. But Hebrews teaches us never to lose sight of the fact that the priesthood, the sacrifices, the liturgy, and the life of the Old Testament church are simply aspects of a rough copy. Christ is the original, the antitype; the pictures of the Old Testament form the type.

## Copies of the Future

This principle is given expression in Hebrews 9:23, which refers to the Old Testament tabernacle, priesthood, and sacrifices as "the copies of the things in the heavens." Yet even more picturesquely, Hebrews 10:1 describes the law as "only a shadow of the good things that are coming" (NIV).

Copies depend on an original. Likewise, a shadow does not exist apart from the person or object whose shadow it is. Both derive their existence and shape from the reality.

## Covenant, Priesthood, and Sacrifice

Hebrews works out this pattern of thought in a series of fascinating ways. The new covenant shapes the old that prepares for it and gives indications of its character and significance. The result is that the old prepares for the new and gives hints of what it will be like.

The priesthood of Christ is the true priesthood that is foreshadowed in the Aaronic priesthood. The inner meaning of the sacrifice of Christ is expressed in a fragmentary way in the Mosaic sacrificial system. But it is clear that these copies are simply that—shadows, hints, outlines—and no more.

The constant repetition of priestly ministry at the altar in the daily sacrifices, the obvious inadequacy of an animal's blood to deal with the blood guilt of a human being—these are hints that the Old Testament arrangement, although divinely commanded, was never intended to be the final one. Something lies beyond it, to which it points; there is a greater, more enduring, more satisfying reality yet to come (cf. Heb. 11:39–12:3).

What is more, by faith the Old Testament believer recognized that this was the case. From Psalm 110:4 he would have been able to see that eternal salvation would need the ministry of someone who was "a priest forever, according to the order of Melchizedek" (Heb. 5:6).

From Psalm 40:6–8 he would have been able to grasp that the final salvation of God would require the obedience of a man (Heb. 10:5ff).

From the daily repetition of sacrifices in Jerusalem he would have been able to see that these were not able to take away his sin fully and finally (Heb. 10:1–4).

From the promise of the new covenant, he would have been able to see that the old arrangement, by which knowing God depended on the mediation of others, would give way one day to a new arrangement. Then all the Lord's people would know Him immediately and intimately (Heb. 8:8–12).

## Eternal Covenant

Tantalizingly, we must read virtually to the end of the letter before all this is put in a nutshell. There we learn that, in His sacrifice, our Lord Jesus Christ shed "the blood of the *everlasting* covenant" (Heb. 13:20). Yes, this means that the covenant will endure forever. But in the light of the rest of the letter, it also means that this new covenant has foundations that are old—indeed, older than the old covenant, reaching back into eternity.

In his famous children's books, C. S. Lewis describes the land of Narnia, which has been placed under a spell by the White Witch. Her magic is deep, creating a world where it is "always winter, but never Christmas." But through the sacrifice of the Lion-King, Aslan, a "deeper magic from before the dawn of time" is released, through which the land is set free from the spell. Time future was prepared for in time past. So it is in the gospel. God had a plan.

Theologians have differed in their ways of describing this plan of salvation designed before "the dawn of time." Sometimes it has been called the covenant of redemption, sometimes the covenant of peace (*pactum salutis*). Theologians as great as Thomas Boston and Jonathan Edwards have disagreed as to whether the plan should properly be described as a covenant at all.

But the debates over nomenclature are incidental to the thing itself. God had a plan, involving the mutual commitment of Father, Son, and Spirit, to save a people. About this the Reformed theologians speak with one voice. The glory in the grace of the gospel is that the triune God, each person in holy and eternal agreement, planned, effected, and applied salvation for you.

## Great Salvation

Before all time; prior to all worlds; when there was nothing "outside of" God Himself; when the Father, Son, and Spirit found eternal, absolute, and unimaginable blessing, pleasure, and joy in Their holy triunity—it was Their agreed purpose to create a world. That world would fall. But in unison—and at infinitely great cost—this glorious triune God planned to bring you (if you are a believer) grace and salvation.

This is deeper grace from before the dawn of time. It was pictured in the rituals, the leaders, and the experiences of the Old Testament saints, all of whom longed to see what we see. All this is now ours. Our salvation depends on God's covenant, rooted in eternity, foreshadowed in the Mosaic liturgy, fulfilled in Christ, enduring forever. No wonder Hebrews calls it "so great a salvation" (Heb. 2:3).

Early in your Christian life, you thought salvation was "great," didn't you? Do you still think about it that way today?

# 29

# THE LIFE OF FAITH

The opening words of Hebrews 11—"Now faith is the substance of things hoped for, the evidence of things not seen"—sometimes perplex Bible students. We are more accustomed to the classical Reformed description of faith as consisting of knowledge, assent, and trust. These biblical words seem to be giving a rather different definition.

What is the explanation? It is a relatively simple one: the author of Hebrews is not analyzing faith into its component parts; instead, he is telling us how faith operates.

## Substance and Evidence

Faith is the substance, that is, the assurance, the steady confidence of mind, even the "title deed" (as one Greek grammar suggests) of that for which we hope.

Here, of course, "hope" ("things hoped for") is not mere wishful thinking. It is certainty about something that is not yet fully realized in our present experience. It is the "hope" of which Paul speaks in Romans 5:5, when he says that the hope of glory will not let us down because we already have tasted the love of God in our hearts through the Spirit.

But faith is also the evidence, that is, the conviction of the reality of what we do not yet see. It is characteristic of the believer who lives "as seeing Him who is invisible" (Heb. 11:27).

Faith, then, in its present activity, is always looking forward to the future. Moreover, exercising it always means that we do not view life and its events through spectacles from the lens-crafters of this world, but through the divine prescription that enables us to have 20/20 spiritual vision on this world because we view it from the perspective of another world.

## Too Heavenly Minded?

This sounds so grand, so deeply theological, that we are surely entitled to ask the author of Hebrews (who tells us he is writing a letter of practical encouragement, 13:22): "What does this mean—if anything!—in practical terms?" Did not Martin Luther say that faith is "a busy, active, mighty thing"?[31] But don't these eloquent expressions point us instead in the direction of the ethereal, the other-worldly, to—in the often-cited put-down—a life that is "too heavenly minded to be of any earthly use"?

On the contrary, the rest of Hebrews 11 is taken up with showing us what this kind of faith means in the nitty-gritty of day-to-day living. The author conducts us on a tour through an amazing portrait gallery of men and women of faith. Only when we reach the end do we realize that he has been leading all along to the person of our Lord Jesus—the originator and completer of faith! His faith also (indeed supremely, as Heb. 12:1ff makes plain) was "the substance of things hoped for, the evidence of things not seen."

These heroes of the faith had two things in common. They looked *beyond the present* to things hoped for and *beyond the visible* to the invisible. They defied the wisdom of the world, which told them to live for today and that what they saw was what was real. Instead, they lived in the present in the light of the future and handled everything that is visible in the light of the invisible.

## Abraham and Moses

There are many Old Testament examples of this, and it is from that portion of the Bible that the author draws all his illustrations of faith. He could hardly have made clearer his conviction about the unity of the Bible, the way of salvation, and the work of the Spirit.

But while Hebrews 11 takes us through thousands of years of the family of faith, it focuses our attention at greater length on two figures—Abraham and Moses. Here were two men who supremely exemplified these twin characteristics of genuine faith.

What was their secret? What explains their wonderful, albeit imperfect, faith? Essentially this: they heard and trusted God's Word or, perhaps even better, they trusted the God who speaks in His Word. It is as simple as this:

*Trust and obey,*
*For there's no other way*
*To be happy in Jesus,*
*But to trust and obey.*[32]

God's word of promise came to Abraham, calling him to leave the visible and the familiar, challenging him to trust a promise to make Abraham a great nation and bring worldwide blessing through his seed, for no other reason than that it was God Himself who gave it. Decades later, that promise scarcely seemed to have reached the starting line. Abraham and Sarah were still a childless couple. But God had promised. However difficult it was to believe His promise in the face of the providence of Sarah's barren womb, Abraham (despite some stumbling) clung on. There is more than one reason for their son to have been called Isaac ("laughter"). He who laughs last laughs longest!

Moses, who entered into the history of that same promise, was told that Yahweh is the covenant promise-making and -keeping God of His people (Ex. 3:1–6; 6:2–9). The suggestion that he—of all people—should lead the vast crowd of enslaved Israelites out of Egypt and into the land promised to Abraham called him to look for a city with different foundations from Rameses in Egypt. He endured much suffering in the visible world because of his conviction about the greater substantiality of the invisible world (and of the Invisible One).

## God's Promises

In other words, to live by faith is not to live by what we can see, feel, and touch—our sense-experience—but on the basis of what God has said and promised. That is faith. It has its epicenter in our Lord Jesus Christ. It takes its practical shape from what God has said and promised in His Word.

It is this, incidentally, that explains why James uses Elijah as an example of the prayer of faith (James 5:15ff). He prayed in faith and the heavens were closed. Three and a half years later, he prayed again and the rains returned.

Elijah did not have famine-creating powers stirring within him. He simply believed God's Word when it promised that if the people were disobedient, Yahweh would send a famine (see Deut. 28:23–24). He—alone it seems—took God's Word at face value.

Faith, as the old hymn says, believes the promises. It is not esoteric, self-serving, or one-up-on in style ("Anything your faith-ministry can do my faith-ministry can do better"). No, faith is simply a matter of knowing what God says, trusting His Word because of who He is, and living in the light of it.

Beware strange ideas of what faith is. People look for the extraordinary or miraculous. But our miracle-working Lord taught, closely followed by Paul (1 Cor. 1:22), that to seek such displays is carnal, not spiritual. Instead, living by faith means doing what the Lord did: living by every word that proceeds from God's mouth (Matt. 4:4, citing Deut. 8:3). It is learning, understanding, embracing, digesting, and applying every last word of Scripture until, as Charles Spurgeon said of the great John Bunyan, if pricked anywhere we would bleed "Bibline."[33]

This is the Bible's key to the life of faith—to be so deeply fed and nourished by the Word of God that it energizes us to live in faith, trusting God's Word, living now in the light of His certain kingdom. From beginning to end, "Faith comes by hearing, and hearing by the word of God" (Rom. 10:17).

This presents an unnerving challenge to us. Know the promises and trust them; know the Word and live on its basis, being guided by its wisdom. Sometimes our problem here, at root, is simply that we do not know our Bibles very well. We are not soaked in, and therefore cannot be energized by, God's Word.

That is a sobering thought for those who would be men and women of faith, is it not?

# 30

# LEANING ON THE PROMISES

O ne of the very first "Christian" possessions I ever had, apart from a Bible, was a "promise box"—a box containing hundreds of biblical promises printed on small cards, one for each day of the year.

I cannot now remember whether my promise box was a gift or a personal purchase. Perhaps my forgetfulness is a personal convenience. It might be something of an embarrassment today to admit to some of my friends that I once bought a promise box! After all, we do not wrest Scripture texts out of their contexts or use the Bible as the ancients used the famous *Sortes Virgilianae*—randomly finding a line from the Roman poet Virgil to guide them on their daily path. To live in this way smacks of a Chinese fortune cookie approach to the Christian life.

God's promises are not fortune cookies. We do not use them in order to get a spiritual "fix" for the day. Serious progress in the Christian life requires the thoughtful understanding of the biblical message as a whole, each part of Scripture understood in its context and applied appropriately to our context. We are, after all, learning to think God's thoughts after Him—about Himself, about the world, about others, about ourselves. God's Word is not a comfort blanket. It is the sword of the Spirit; indeed, it is sharper than any two-edged sword (Heb. 4:12).

All this is true. But the other day I remembered my long-lost promise box, and I found myself asking the question: Did I throw out the baby with the bathwater? Do I still have a firm grasp on the promises the Lord has given me, and am I still living on that basis day by day? What promises have

I seen Him fulfilling for me recently? What promises am I expecting Him to keep in my life?

## Promises and Holiness

There are two places in particular in the New Testament where right living is seen as the direct consequence of trusting God's promises.

Writes Paul to the Corinthians: "Since we have these promises . . . let us cleanse ourselves from every defilement of body and spirit . . ." (2 Cor. 7:1, ESV).

The "promises" to which Paul refers here are God's covenant commitments to His people that He will be with them, receive those who "touch no unclean thing," and be a Father to them (2 Cor. 6:16–18, ESV). Paul reasons that if this is what God promises to be to His holy people, we should make every effort to be such holy people. If these are the riches that await me, let me walk on that path of holiness that leads to them. Here holiness is a direct result of living in the light of the divine promises.

Peter writes in a similar vein: "[God] has given us his very great and precious promises, so that through them you may participate in the divine nature and escape the corruption in the world caused by evil desires" (2 Peter 1:4, NIV). Here, the promises of God in general are in view. What is their fruit? Once again it is holiness, or right living.

This raises a question: What promises of God have been etched on my heart? What am I expectantly waiting to receive from the Father of lights who does not change like shifting shadows (James 1:17)? Am I really living as His covenant child, with the words, "Father, you promised . . ." forming on my lips, as I live in expectation of Him keeping His word?

## Living in the Promise

How am I to live my life in the light of God's promises?

First of all, I must know what God's promises are.

The old daily Bible study question was not far off the mark when it asked, "Is there a promise here for me today?" We may need to outgrow the "promise box mentality," but we can never outgrow the promises themselves. Scripture is full of them. Ask yourself: Is there one in the passage of Scripture I read today? Did I even read a passage of Scripture today?

Second, I must feed my mind on the promises of God. As a child I often was amazed by the ability of a member of my grandparents' generation to suck a single peppermint for a half-hour, while mine was crunched to pieces within minutes! We need to learn to suck the flavors from God's Word, slowly savoring God's promises, metaphorically placing them "under our tongue," allowing them to release their pleasurable blessings over the whole day. We need to meditate on them if we are to find them redirecting our thinking and filling us with an expectation that the Lord will keep His word. Only then will we be able to say, "How sweet are your words to my taste" (Ps. 119:103, NIV).

Third, I must let God's promises govern my lifestyle. Has He promised never to leave me? Then I will commune with Him regularly, as an expression of my faith that He is near. I will allow the knowledge of His presence to give me poise in times of crisis and pressure. I will live in such a way that I will not be ashamed that He is near.

It is not surprising that Peter speaks about "great and precious promises." He had clung fiercely to Christ's promise when everything within him and around him seemed to be caving in. Jesus had said: "I have prayed for you, Simon, that your faith may not fail. And when you have turned back . . ." (Luke 22:32, NIV). Peter's hope in Christ's implicit promise of his restoration was the very reason he had held on.

May God's promises similarly renew your life.

# 31

# THE PRAYER OF FAITH

Years ago, the editor of a publishing company asked me to write a book on prayer. The theme is a vitally important one. The publishing house was well known. To be honest, I felt flattered. But in a moment of heaven-sent honesty, I told him that the author of such a book would need to be an older and more seasoned author (not to mention, alas, more prayerful) than I was. I mentioned one name and then another. My reaction seemed to encourage him to a moment of honesty, as well. He smiled. He had already asked the well-seasoned Christian leaders whose names I had just mentioned! They, too, had declined in similar terms. Wise men, I thought. Who can write or speak at any length easily on the mystery of prayer?

Yet in the past century and a half, much has been written and said particularly about "the prayer of faith." The focus has been on mountain-moving prayer by which we simply "claim" things from God with confidence that we will receive them because we believe that He will give them.

But what exactly is the prayer of faith?

## *Association with the Dramatic*

Interestingly, it is in the letter of James (who has so much to say about *works*) that the term occurs. It climaxes the marvelous teaching on prayer that punctuates the entire letter (see 1:5–8; 4:2–3; 5:13–18).

What is even more striking is that the significance of the phrase seems to be illustrated by the experience of one individual, the prophet Elijah. In his case, the prayer of faith was instrumental in shutting the heavens. Perhaps it is not surprising, therefore, that the phrase has come to be associated largely, if not exclusively, with dramatic, miracle-like events—with the extraordinary rather than the daily.

Yet this misses the basic thrust of James's teaching. The reason Elijah is used as an example is not that he was an extraordinary man; James stresses that he was "a man with a nature like ours" (James 5:17). It is his ordinariness that is in view.

Elijah's praying is used as an example not because it produced miracle-like effects but because it gives us one of the clearest of all illustrations of what it means for anyone to pray with faith: it is believing God's revealed Word, taking hold of His covenant commitment to it, and asking Him to keep it.

## The Prayer of a Righteous Person

Shutting up the heavens was not, after all, a novel idea that originated in the fertile mind of Elijah. In fact, it was the fulfillment of the promised curse of the covenant Lord: "If you do not obey the LORD your God . . . these curses will come upon you. . . . The LORD will strike you . . . with scorching heat and drought. . . . The sky over your head will be bronze, the ground beneath you iron. The LORD will turn the rain of your country into dust and powder" (Deut. 28:15, 22–24, NIV).

Like every "righteous man" (James 5:16), Elijah sought to align his life with God's covenant promises and threats (which is, essentially, what "righteousness" means in the Old Testament—to be rightly covenantally related to the Lord). He lived his life in the light of the covenant God had made, and so he held on to its threats of judgment in prayer, as well as to its promises of blessing.

This, then, is the prayer of faith: to ask God to accomplish what He has promised in His Word. That promise is the only ground for our confidence in asking. Such confidence is not "worked up" from within our emotional life; rather, it is given and supported by what God has said in Scripture.

Truly "righteous" men and women of faith know the value of their heavenly Father's promises. They go to Him, as children do to a loving human father. They know that if they can say to an earthly father, "But, father, you promised . . . ," they can both persist in asking and be confident that he will keep his word. How much more our heavenly Father, who has given His Son for our salvation! We have no other grounds of confidence that He hears our prayers. We need none.

## Legitimate Prayer

Such appeal to God's promises constitutes what John Calvin, following Tertullian, calls "legitimate prayer."[34]

Some Christians find this disappointing. It seems to remove the mystique from the prayer of faith. Are we not tying down our faith to ask only for what God already has promised? But such disappointment reveals a spiritual malaise: would we rather devise our own spirituality (preferably spectacular) than God's (frequently modest)?

The struggles we sometimes experience in prayer, then, are often part of the process by which God gradually brings us to ask for only what He has promised to give. The struggle is not our wrestling to bring Him to give us what we desire, but our wrestling with His Word until we are illuminated and subdued by it, saying, "Not my will, but Your will be done." Then, as Calvin again says, we learn "not to ask for more than God allows."[35]

This is why true prayer can never be divorced from real holiness. The prayer of faith can be made only by the "righteous" man whose life is being more and more aligned with the covenant grace and purposes of God. In the realm of prayer, too (since it is a microcosm of the whole of the Christian life), faith (prayer to the covenant Lord) without works (obedience to the covenant Lord) is dead.

# 32

# "The Greatest of All Protestant Heresies"?

Let us begin with a church history exam question: *Complete, explain, and discuss this statement*: "The greatest of all Protestant heresies is . . ." (Robert Bellarmine).

Cardinal Robert Bellarmine (1542–1621) was a figure not to be taken lightly. He was Pope Clement VIII's personal theologian and one of the most able figures in the Counter-Reformation movement within sixteenth-century Roman Catholicism.

How would you answer the exam question? What is the greatest of all Protestant heresies? Perhaps justification by faith? Perhaps Scripture alone, or one of the other Reformation watchwords?

Those answers make perfectly good and logical sense. But none of them completes Bellarmine's sentence.

He wrote: "The greatest of all Protestant heresies is *assurance*."

A moment's reflection explains why. If justification is not by faith *alone*, in Christ *alone*, by grace *alone*; if faith needs to be completed by works; if Christ's sacrifice is somehow repeated or needs to be re-presented; if grace is not free and sovereign—then something always needs be "added" for final justification to be ours.

That is exactly the problem. If final justification is dependent on something we have to complete, it is not possible to enjoy assurance of salvation. For then final justification is contingent and uncertain. How can anyone be sure he or she has done enough? In Bellarmine's view, only someone who has attained great holiness and who has received special personal revelation—a true saint such as Thomas Aquinas, perhaps—can experience assurance.

But if Christ has done everything; if justification is by grace, without contributory works; if it is received by faith's empty hands—then assurance, even full assurance, is possible *for every believer.*

No wonder Bellarmine thought full, free, unfettered grace was dangerous!

No wonder the Reformers loved the letter to the Hebrews!

The anonymous author of Hebrews pauses for breath at the climax of his exposition of Christ's work (Heb. 10:18), then continues his argument with a Paul-like "therefore" (10:19). He urges us to "draw near . . . in *full assurance of faith*" (10:22).

We do not need to re-read the whole letter to see the logical power of this "therefore." Christ is our High Priest, and our hearts have been sprinkled from an evil conscience just as our bodies have been washed with pure water (v. 22). Therefore. . . .

What does this mean, in plain terms?


## Good Things to Come

In Hebrews, our Lord already has been described as the "High Priest of the good things to come" (9:11), things represented in shadow form under the old covenant (10:1). "Good things" (*agatha*) was a term often associated by Jews with the Promised Land and its blessings (a land of abundance, blessing, and joy, "flowing with milk and honey").

Throughout Old Testament times, God's people realized that this land contained only glimpses and tastes of these good things (see Heb. 11:14–16, 39–40). They experienced them the way an infant, seated in a baby chair, "tastes" food, in puree form. Only much later will the baby sit at the family table to enjoy the pleasures of an entire meal. The child may sometimes bang his spoon in frustration, but he cannot yet fully experience "the good things" to come!

In the same way, Old Testament believers saw the gospel in the shadow-lands of the law. They caught a glimpse of the coming Savior in the representative figure of the high priest, and looked to the coming sacrifice to which the daily and annual sacrifices pointed. This was to experience the grace of God in infancy, as it were. But now the long-awaited good things have come. The early morning shadows of dawn have given way to the bright light of the day. Nothing now stands between the believer and the Lord: not temple, not priest, not sacrifice—nothing.

## Final Sacrifice, Full Salvation

Christ has become the once-for-all sacrifice for our sins. He has been raised and vindicated in the power of an indestructible life as our representative priest. By faith in Him, we are as righteous before the throne of God as He is. For we are justified in His righteousness; His justification before God is ours! And we can no more lose this justification than He can fall from heaven. Thus, our justification does not need to be completed any more than does Christ's! It is complete already, and it is permanent.

With this in view, the author says that "by one offering He *has perfected forever* those who are being sanctified" (Heb. 10:14).

## Blessed Assurance

We can stand before God in full assurance because we now experience "hearts sprinkled from an evil conscience and . . . bodies washed with pure water" (Heb. 10:22). Perhaps the writer is speaking here about the reality of forgiveness and its sign (baptism), or perhaps (using hendiadys, the method of describing one reality in two different aspects) "hearts . . . bodies" here refers to the whole person.

In either case, the point is clear enough. When I know that Christ is the one real sacrifice for my sins, that His work on my behalf has been accepted by God, that He is my heavenly Intercessor—then His blood is the antidote to the poison in the voices that echo in my conscience, condemning me for my many failures. Indeed, Christ's shed blood chokes them into silence!

Thus, knowing that Jesus Christ is my Savior delivers me from my anxious fears, and brings me joy and wonderful assurance. I am condemned no more—not even by my own conscience. Jesus is mine. Blessed assurance indeed!

## *Practical Outworking*

"Ah," retorted Cardinal Bellarmine's Rome, "teach this and those who believe it will live in license and antinomianism."

But listen instead to the logic of Hebrews. Enjoying this assurance leads to:

1. Unwavering faithfulness to our confession of faith in Jesus Christ alone as our hope (Heb. 10:23).

2. Careful consideration of how we can encourage each other to "love and good works" (v. 24).

3. Ongoing communion with other Christians in worship, fellowship, and service (v. 25a).

4. A life in which we exhort one another to keep looking to Christ and to be faithful to Him, as the time of His return draws ever nearer (v. 25b).

It is the good tree that produces good fruit, not the other way around. We are not saved *by* works, but we are saved *for* works. In fact, we are God's workmanship at work (Eph. 2:9–10)! Thus, rather than lead a life of moral and spiritual indifference, believers have the most powerful impetus for the ongoing work of living to God's glory and pleasure—the once-for-all work of Jesus Christ and the full assurance of faith it produces.

Furthermore, this full assurance is rooted in the fact that God has done all this for us. He has revealed His heart to us in Christ. The Father did not require the death of Christ to persuade Him to love us. Christ died *because* the Father loves us (John 3:16). The Father of Glory does not lurk behind His Son with sinister intent to do us ill, restrained only by the cruel and bloody sacrifice His Son has made! No, a thousand times no! The Father loves us in the love of the Son and the love of the Spirit (John 16:27).

Those who enjoy such assurance do not go to the saints or to Mary. Those who look to Jesus need look nowhere else. In Him we enjoy full assurance of salvation.

Assurance the greatest of all heresies? If so, let me enjoy this most blessed of "heresies"! For it is God's own truth and grace!

# PART V

# A Life
# of Wisdom

*The Bible urges us not only to grow in knowledge but to "Get wisdom!" (Prov. 4:5). True, we must grow in knowledge. But wise Christians do not simply understand the gospel; their lifestyles are wonderful expressions of the melody of the gospel.*

# 33

# PRIVILEGES BRING RESPONSIBILITIES

The letter to the Hebrews is full of Old Testament language and ritual. Running through it is a sense that as believers we are on the move, on a pilgrimage through the wilderness. This motif echoes in our ears as we turn the pages. We are seeking to reach the land of rest (4:1) and striving to enter it (4:11). Indeed, we are aiming to draw near to the throne of its King (4:16; 10:19). It is the throne of grace before which Christ our High Priest stands. So we run the race that will bring us there with perseverance, our eyes fixed on Him (12:1–2).

All this lies behind the remarkable words of Hebrews 12:18–29. It is not to Mount Sinai that we have come, as Moses and the first pilgrim people did. We are participants in the new exodus accomplished by Christ (Luke 9:31, where "decease" or "departure" is, literally, *exodus*). We have come to Mount Zion, the heavenly Jerusalem. We have already received a kingdom that cannot be shaken (12:28). That is why we must see to it that we "do not refuse Him who speaks" (12:25; the present tense is interesting and significant; Scripture is God's living voice addressing us; cf. 12:5).

This sustained use of Old Testament exodus imagery is all-pervasive in Hebrews. But the underlying structures of thought are the same as elsewhere in the New Testament:

1. The promise of the old has been fulfilled in the new, in Christ.

In addition, another grammatical pattern is evident, one we usually associate with the apostle Paul:

2. The indicatives of grace (God has shown His grace in Christ) provide the foundation for the imperatives of obedience (now we are called to live for Christ's glory).

Indeed, this principle is also evident in the way in which:

3. Christians are urged to live in the light of the privileges they enjoy already and therefore to persevere to enter those they do not yet fully experience.

Thus:

- *Promise* leads to *fulfillment.*
- *Grace* leads to *obedience.*
- *Already* is linked to *not yet.*

As the author comes to the final "warning passage" in Hebrews (12:25–29), it helps to see its apparent severity in the light of this third principle.

## Coming to an Abiding City

What are our privileges? They are truly amazing. "For you have not come to what may be touched, a blazing fire and darkness and gloom and a tempest. . . . But you have come to Mount Zion and to the city of the living God, the heavenly Jerusalem, and to innumerable angels in festal gathering" (Heb. 12:18, 22, ESV).

In the days of promises and shadows, believers came to an assembly convened at a mountain engulfed with a sense of awful judgment. By contrast, in the full blaze of light that has appeared in Christ, we have come to the abiding city of God, angels in festal gathering, the assembly of Christ, and the spirits of departed believers. Indeed, we have come to God Himself, not with Moses, but to Jesus. We have received the new covenant in His shed blood.

## Every Service

This is the *assembly* in which we gather for worship to hear the voice of Christ in His Word, to lift our voices under His choral direction in praise, to share His trust in His Father, and to gather around Him as His brothers and sisters (cf. Heb. 2:10–13). Consequently, this is also our *family*—composed of the redeemed from among all mankind and the elect among the angelic host. This is the *kingdom* in which our names are enrolled as citizens (12:23). It is a kingdom, unlike all the kingdoms and empires of this world, that cannot be shaken (12:27–28).

What riches are ours in these three dimensions of the life of grace! An assembly, a family, a kingdom! *And they are already ours in Christ!* Here and now our lives are punctuated by special visiting rights to heaven's glory as we assemble with our fellow believers. We are brothers and sisters together—for Christ's blood creates a deeper lineage than our genes. Thus, we have the full rights of family members and citizens in the city of God.

No wonder we should be grateful (12:28)!

## Positives and Negatives

As noted above, this is the last of several extended warning passages in Hebrews. Some of them often have been regarded as particularly problematic passages because of the implication they seem to carry, namely that believers might fall away from Christ and be lost.

But to read them thus is to abstract them from their context in the letter and from the covenant dynamic of the gospel.

The warning passages in Hebrews belong to an ongoing series of exhortations to be read in the light of the privileges of grace. In fact, the author thinks of his entire letter as a "word of exhortation" or encouragement to persevere (13:22). As any father would do, this spiritual father, speaking on behalf of the "Father of spirits" (12:9), encourages his spiritual children with exhortations that are both positive and negative:

**Positive:** "Give the more earnest heed . . ."; **negative:** ". . . lest we drift" (2:1).

**Positive:** "Consider . . . Christ Jesus" (3:1); **negative:** "Beware, brethren . . ." (3:12), and so on until we come to this final section:

**Positive:** "You have come to Mount Zion . . ." (12:22); **negative:** "See that you do not refuse Him who speaks" (12:25).

This is all of a piece with the loving father who tells his son that a well-rounded diet and exercise will contribute to good health, but bad eating habits, cigarette-smoking, and over-indulgence in strong spirits coupled with a couch-potato lifestyle are calculated to induce premature death.

### Covenant Structure

The key here is the new covenant structure of the gospel. It is built on a better Mediator and better promises than the old. But it remains a covenant. Its dynamic is the same: God gives His promise of grace (fulfilled now in Christ), a promise of life through faith in Christ, but also of death outside of Christ for any who spurn the blood of the new covenant (cf. 10:26–31).

God's covenant is not a container that encloses us no matter how we live. It is, rather, the sure promise of God that He will save those who take hold of Christ in faith and repentance, with the corresponding certainty that if we reject Him in unbelief and disobedience, spurning the covenant of Christ, then we are already on the road that leads only to the outer darkness.

Faith and repentance are not static, the decision of a moment; they are the lifelong realities of a new heart (8:10; 10:16). Yes, our faith and repentance have a starting point, but it is the beginning of a pilgrimage we share with the community of the new covenant. If we do not walk in faith and repentance, we may be among the visible people of Christ, but we are not a living part of them because we never mix the promise of God with faith (Heb. 4:2).

So we *already* "have come to Mount Zion . . . the heavenly Jerusalem." But we have *not yet* finally entered it. We hear its worship; we experience its power; its light illumines our camping ground (Heb. 6:4–5). The doors of the city are never shut (Rev. 21:25), but we do not yet dwell inside the city gates. There is a river still to be crossed. God's covenant faithfulness calls for faith that perseveres to the end.

When we have seen the privileges that are already ours, we have every reason to keep our eyes fixed on Jesus and persevere in penitential faith until that which is now ours in part becomes ours in whole and forever.

# 34

# WHERE GOD LOOKS FIRST

W
ho are you behind closed doors?

You may have heard these words (or some variation on them) quoted before: "What a man is in secret, in these private duties, that he is in the eyes of God and no more."[36] The most frequently quoted version is usually attributed to the young Scotsman, Robert Murray McCheyne. But other masters of the Christian way have echoed these sentiments.

Perhaps they borrowed unconsciously from one another; more likely, they all learned the same lessons the hard way—by personal experience. In any event, they all came to see the same three elements to be vital for right Christian living.

### *Hidden Devotion*

First, they learned that it is in secret, not in public, that what we really are as Christians becomes clear. It is not my visible service so much as my hidden life of devotion that is the index of my spirituality. That is not to despise my public life, but to anchor its reality to the ocean bed of personal fellowship with God. I may speak or pray with zeal and eloquence in public. I may appear to others to be master of myself when in company. But what happens when I close the door behind myself and only the Father sees me?

In the Sermon on the Mount, Jesus warned His disciples against hypocrisy before men and encouraged them to be transparent before God.

How easily in our culture we are deceived into thinking that it is what is seen in public that really matters. How curious it would have seemed to the apostles that the services of worship in which we can so easily be visible spectators are so much better attended than our meetings for closed-eye prayer. Will the bubble of our visible success ever burst?

Occasionally the statistics indicate how great is the gap between the image we present as evangelicals and the reality that we mask. We do not always exercise "sincere faith" (1 Tim. 1:5; *pistis anupokritos*—unhypocritical faith, faith that does not need the actor's mask). Life has a way of ripping off the mask to reveal what is really there.

Just as abuse of or inattention to the body reveals itself in older age, so does the abuse of the spirit. Inevitably it manifests itself in stunted, ill-disciplined, or twisted character. The Father has a way of rewarding us openly— one way or another (Matt. 6:5–6). Therefore, live well in secret; be molded by Scripture; learn to pray; and control your thought life by God's grace.

## *Duty as Delight*

Second, the past masters of the Christian life stressed that it is not lived on the basis of our feelings but in fulfilling duties. Sanctification is not a mood condition, but the submission of our wills to the will of God.

In recent decades, evangelicalism has become so sensitive to the heresy of "Boy Scout Christianity" ("I promise to do my best, to do my duty . . .") that it has truncated the Christian gospel to a half-Christ (Savior, but not Lord) and a half-salvation (blessings, but not duties). How foolish we have been, when so much of the New Testament catalogs the specific duties that arise out of our relationship to Jesus Christ and therefore are in fact among our blessings.

A survey of a few passages in the Epistles will exorcise the demon of thinking that duty is alien to Christian living or to Christian love. Just look at Romans 12:1–15; Galatians 5:13–6:10; Ephesians 4:1–6:20; Philippians 4:2–9; Colossians 3:1–4:6; 1 Thessalonians 4:1–5:28; 2 Thessalonians 2:13–15; James 1:19–5:20; and 1 Peter 1:13–5:11. Doubtless some scholar somewhere has counted the number of imperatives ("Do so-and-so") in the New Testament. Every one of them matters; every one of them grows out of God's grace; every one of them was written to be obeyed.

Are we frightened that fulfilling our duties will overturn the grace of God? Look at the busy housewife whose entire life is governed by her multifaceted responsibilities. While her husband enters his own world (often exciting and challenging), she makes the lunches, drives the children to school, shops, cleans, washes, irons, mends, prepares the meals, cleans up, and gets the children to bed. Why? Duty. These are the duties of love, devotion, and commitment.

Love for God and duty are two parts of the same thing. How foolish we have been to separate them and to regard *duty* as a bad word. It nourishes Christlikeness (John 4:34). Therefore, know your Christian duties and fulfill them.

## Coram Deo

Third, these masters learned to live visibly, even in secret. They lived *coram Deo* (before the face of God). That one principle is enough to transform the whole of life and to rid us of all attempts at deception—of others, of God, of self. Nothing is hidden from the eyes of Him with whom we have to do (Heb. 4:13).

Has that thought sufficiently gripped my mind and begun to dominate my every action, producing the quality of transparency in my life? It is the one sure way to enjoy liberty from the pressures of the world to conform to its mold, and to overcome the fear of man. Those who make it their aim to have a conscience void of offense before God are Christ's free men. Therefore, live the whole of your life as in the presence of God.

Here, then, are three tests that provide a good measure of where I am spiritually:

1. What am I really like in secret?
2. How do I react to the word *duty*?
3. Am I living with a sense of how visible my life is to God?

Incidentally, the version of the evangelical dictum quoted above comes from John Owen. He suggests that to fail to deal with these issues in the heart is like leaving "a moth in a garment, to eat up and devour the stringed threads of it, so that though the whole hang loose together, it is easily torn to pieces."[37]

Wise words indeed!

# DISCERNMENT:
# THINKING GOD'S THOUGHTS

Someone I know recently expressed an opinion that surprised and in some ways disappointed me. I said to myself, "I thought he would have more discernment than that."

The experience caused me to reflect on the importance of discernment and the lack of it in our world. We know that people often do not see issues clearly and are easily misled because they do not think biblically. But, sadly, one cannot help reflecting on how true this is of the church community, too.

Most of us doubtless want to distance ourselves from what might be regarded as "the lunatic fringe" of contemporary Christianity. We are on our guard against being led astray by false teachers. But there is more to discernment than this. True discernment means not only distinguishing the right from the wrong; it means distinguishing the primary from the secondary, the essential from the indifferent, and the permanent from the transient. And, yes, it means distinguishing between the good and the better, and even between the better and the best.

Thus, discernment is like the physical senses; to some it is given in unusual measure as a special grace gift (1 Cor. 12:10), but some measure of it is essential for us all and must be constantly nourished. The Christian must take care to develop his "sixth sense" of spiritual discernment. This is why the psalmist prays, "Teach me *good judgment* and knowledge" (Ps. 119:66).

## The Nature of Discernment

But what is this discernment? The word used in Psalm 119:66 means "taste." It is the ability to make discriminating judgments, to distinguish between, and recognize the moral implications of, different situations and courses of action. It includes the ability to "weigh up" and assess the moral and spiritual status of individuals, groups, and even movements. Thus, while warning us against judgmental*ism*, Jesus urges us to be discerning and discriminating, lest we cast our pearls before pigs (Matt. 7:1, 6).

A remarkable example of such discernment is described in John 2:24–25: "Jesus would not entrust himself to them . . . for he knew what was in a man" (NIV).

This is discernment without judgmentalism. It involved our Lord's knowledge of God's Word *and* His observation of God's ways with men (He, supremely, had prayed, "Teach me good judgment . . . for I believe Your commandments," Ps. 119:66). Doubtless His discernment grew as He experienced conflict with, and victory over, temptation, and as He assessed every situation in the light of God's Word.

Jesus' discernment penetrated to the deepest reaches of the heart. But the Christian is called to develop similar discernment. For the only worthwhile discernment we possess is that which we receive in union with Christ, by the Spirit, through God's Word.

So discernment is learning to think God's thoughts after Him, practically and spiritually; it means having a sense of how things look in God's eyes and seeing them in some measure "uncovered and laid bare" (Heb. 4:13).

## The Impact of Discernment

How does this discernment affect the way we live? In four ways:

1. It acts as a means of protection, guarding us from being deceived spiritually. It protects us from being blown away by the winds of teaching that make central an element of the gospel that is peripheral or treat a particular application of Scripture as though it were Scripture's central message.

2. Discernment also acts as an instrument of healing, when exercised in grace. I have known a small number of people whose ability to diagnose the spiritual needs of others has been remarkable. Such people seem able to penetrate into the heart issues someone else faces better than the person can do. Of course, this is in some ways a dangerous gift with which God has entrusted them. But when exercised in love, discernment can be the surgical scalpel in spiritual surgery that makes healing possible.

3. Again, discernment functions as a key to Christian freedom. The zealous but undiscerning Christian becomes enslaved—to others, to his own uneducated conscience, to an unbiblical pattern of life. Growth in discernment sets us free from such bondage, enabling us to distinguish practices that may be helpful in some circumstances from those that are mandated in all circumstances. But in another way, true discernment enables the free Christian to recognize that the exercise of freedom is not essential to the enjoyment of it.

4. Finally, discernment serves as a catalyst to spiritual development: "The mocker seeks wisdom and finds none, but knowledge comes easily to the discerning" (Prov. 14:6, NIV). Why? Because the discerning Christian goes to the heart of the matter. He knows something about everything, namely that all things have their common fountain in God. Increase in knowledge, therefore, does not lead to increased frustration, but to a deeper recognition of the harmony of all God's works and words.

How is such discernment to be obtained? We receive it as did Christ Himself—by the anointing of the Spirit, through our understanding of God's Word, by our experience of God's grace, and by the progressive unfolding to us of the true condition of our own hearts.

That is why we also should pray, "I am your servant; give me discernment" (Ps. 119:125, NIV).

# 36

# GOD'S
# MYSTERIOUS WILL

An encounter with a friend from my teenage years reminded me of the wise and pithy words of the Puritan writer John Flavel: "The providence of God is like Hebrew words—it can be read only backwards."[38]

I was leaving a restaurant in my native city in Scotland one day, and there was my friend being helped along by his elderly mother. His had been one of those active, energized, intense spirits. He was the one who had given me the first Christian books that ever made a real impression on me, who had poured out his own life-energy to befriend me and teach me. Now his condition was just as someone had hinted to me—his powers had been wasted by a serious auto accident.

To my intense delight, he recognized me, and for a moment the old energy seemed to surge into his being. Just as quickly it subsided, like a lightbulb fusing in the moment of illumination. It was as though the sight of a friend from the past had deceivingly invigorated him, only to remind him immediately of his terrible infirmity.

His gesticulations had always been one of his chief characteristics. Now the movements of his hands and body, and the look in his eyes, all created a wistful melody in the minor key.

## *Footsteps in the Sea*

Of this and other experiences in life, I have sometimes thought, "It just does not seem to make sense."

At such times, Flavel's words have often comforted me and helped me to readjust my myopic spiritual perspective. They have reminded me to fix my mind and heart on God's wise, gracious, and sovereign rule, and on the assurance that He works everything together for His children's good, so that I do not inquire too proudly into why I cannot understand His sovereign purposes.

Of course, one occasionally meets Christians for whom the Lord's purposes are "all sewn up." They convey an attitude of knowing exactly what He is doing and why He is doing it. Such comprehensive wisdom is difficult to dislodge, but it is often the precocious wisdom of the immature Christian who has not yet learned that while "those things which are revealed belong to us and to our children," there are also hidden and secret things that "belong to the LORD our God" (Deut. 29:29).

God's ways and thoughts are not ours. We never have them "taped." As William Cowper knew well, God "plants his footsteps in the sea."[39] We can no more read in detail God's secret purposes for our individual lives than we can see footsteps in water or understand Hebrew if we try to read it from left to right. To imagine we can is to suffer from a form of spiritual dyslexia.

One great reason for this principle is to teach us to "Trust in the LORD with all [our] heart, and lean not on [our] own understanding" (Prov. 3:5). So perverse are we that we would use our knowledge of God's will to substitute for actual daily personal trust in the Lord Himself.

Flavel's Law (if we may so speak of his wise words) has widespread relevance for Christian living, but is particularly important in four ways:

## *The Big Decisions*

It is true of the big decisions of life. God does guide His people, leading them in the right paths (Ps. 23:3). It is a great thing to come to a major decision with the assurance that it is His will. But we would be mistaken to imagine that we therefore know in detail the reasons behind His plan.

Many Christians have discovered that obedience to what they believed to be God's will led to great personal difficulties. When this happens to us, it is only later that we discover that God's purpose in leading us to a new orientation or situation may have been very different from the extrapolation we made from the first points we saw on the divine graph of our lives.

## The Tests

It is true of the tests of life. We struggle to endure them for what they are in themselves. Afterward, we are relieved to have them at our back.

But in fact, earlier testing is often designed to strengthen us for later trials. Only when we have been brought through the later ones do the earlier ones more fully "make sense."

## The Tragedies

It is true of the tragedies of life. We will not fully see their place in the divine economy in this world. Their ultimate explanation lies beyond our personal lives and even beyond time.

Think, for example, of Naomi's triple bereavement in Ruth 1, and how that led, in the slow unfolding of God's purpose, to Ruth's conversion, marriage, and motherhood; the coming of David; and finally the birth of Christ.

I have no special insight into God's purpose in the life of my friend, but that He has a gracious purpose is beyond doubt, however opaque it seems at present.

## The Whole

It is true of the whole of life. As C. S. Lewis illuminatingly put it, only when someone has died do we see his or her life in its completeness. But even then we catch only a fleeting glimpse of what will finally be made manifest. The ultimate unfolding awaits the day when "I shall know fully, even as I am fully known" (1 Cor. 13:12, NIV).

Has it ever struck you that our Lord's words in the upper room had long-term as well as short-term significance? "You do not realize now what I am doing, but later you will understand" (John 13:7, NIV).

# 37

# EATING BLACK PUDDING

I t was years ago now, but I still remember the discussion. I was making my way out of our church building some time after the morning service had ended, and was surprised to find a small group of people still engaged in vigorous conversation. One of them turned and said to me, "Can Christians eat black pudding?"

To the uninitiated in the mysteries of Scottish haute cuisine, it should perhaps be said that black pudding is not haggis! It is a sausage made of blood and suet, sometimes with flour or meal.

It seems a trivial question. Why the vigorous debate? Because, of course, of the Old Testament's regulations about eating blood (Lev. 17:10ff).

Although (as far as I am aware) no theological dictionary contains an entry under B for "The Black Pudding Controversy," this unusual discussion raised some most basic hermeneutical and theological issues:

- How is the Old Testament related to the New?
- How is the Law of Moses related to the gospel of Jesus Christ?
- How should a Christian exercise freedom in Christ?

The Council of Jerusalem, described in Acts 15, sought to answer such practical questions faced by the early Christians as they wrestled with how to enjoy freedom from the Mosaic administration without becoming stumbling blocks to Jewish people.

These were questions to which Paul in particular gave a great deal of thought. He was, after all, one of those appointed by the Jerusalem Council to circulate and explain the letter that summarized the decisions of the apostles and elders (Acts 15:22ff; 16:4). Faced with similar issues in the church at Rome, he provided them with a series of principles that apply equally well to twenty-first-century Christians. His teaching in Romans 14:1–15:13 contains healthy (and very necessary) guidelines for the exercise of Christian liberty. Here are four of them:

**Principle 1:** Christian liberty must never be flaunted. "Whatever you believe about these things keep between yourself and God" (Rom. 14:22, NIV).

We are free in Christ from the Mosaic dietary laws; Christ has pronounced all food clean (Mark 7:18–19). We may eat black pudding after all!

*But you do not need to exercise your liberty in order to enjoy it.* Indeed, Paul elsewhere asks some very penetrating questions of those who insist on exercising their liberty whatever the circumstances: Does this really build up others? Is this really liberating you—or has it actually begun to enslave you (Rom. 14:19; 1 Cor. 6:12)?

The subtle truth is that the Christian who *has to* exercise his or her liberty is in bondage to the very thing he or she insists on doing. Says Paul, if the kingdom consists for you in food, drink, and the like, you have missed the point of the gospel and the freedom of the Spirit (Rom. 14:17).

**Principle 2:** Christian liberty does not mean that you welcome fellow Christians only when you have sorted out their views on X or Y (or with a view to doing that).

God has welcomed them in Christ, as they are; so should we (Rom. 14:1, 3). True, the Lord will not leave them as they are. But He does not make their pattern of conduct the basis of His welcome. Neither should we.

We have many responsibilities for our fellow Christians, but being their judge is not one of them. Christ alone is that (Rom. 14:4, 10–13). How sad it is to hear (as we do far too often) the name of another Christian mentioned in conversation, only for someone to pounce immediately on him or her in criticism. That is not so much a mark of discernment as it is the evidence of a judgmental spirit.

What if the measure we use to judge others becomes the measure used to judge us (Rom. 14:10–12; Matt. 7:2)?

**Principle 3:** Christian liberty ought never to be used in such a way that you become a stumbling block to another Christian (Rom. 14:13).

When Paul states this principle, it is not a spur-of-the-moment reaction, but a settled principle he has thought out and to which he has very deliberately committed himself (see 1 Cor. 8:13). When that commitment is made, it eventually becomes so much a part of our thinking that it directs our behavior instinctively. We are given liberty in Christ in order to be the servants of others, not in order to indulge our own preferences.

**Principle 4:** Christian liberty requires grasping the principle that will produce this true biblical balance: "We . . . ought . . . not to please ourselves. . . . For even Christ did not please himself" (Rom. 15:1–3).

There is something devastatingly simple about this. It reduces the issue to the basic questions of love for the Lord Jesus Christ and a desire to imitate Him since His Spirit indwells us to make us more like Him.

True Christian liberty, unlike the various "freedom" or "liberation" movements of the secular world, is not a matter of demanding the "rights" we have. Dare one say that the American Founding Fathers, for all their wisdom, may have inadvertently triggered off a distortion of Christianity by speaking about our "rights" to life, liberty, and the pursuit of happiness? The Christian realizes that before God he or she possesses no "rights" by nature. In our sinfulness, we have forfeited all of our "rights."

Only when we recognize that we do not deserve our "rights" can we properly exercise them as privileges. Sensitivity to others in the church, especially weaker others, depends on this sense of our own unworthiness. If we assume that we have liberties to be exercised at all costs, we become potentially lethal weapons in a fellowship, all too capable of destroying someone for whom Christ has died (Rom. 14:15, 20).

That does not mean that I must become the slave of another's conscience. John Calvin puts the point well when he says that we restrain the exercise of our freedom for the sake of weak believers, but not when we are faced with Pharisees who demand that we conform to what is unscriptural.[40] Where the gospel is at stake, liberty needs to be exercised; where the stability of a weak Christian is at stake, we need to restrain it.

This is all part and parcel of "living between the times." Already, in Christ, we are free, but we do not yet live in a world that can cope with our freedom. One day we will enjoy "the glorious liberty of the children of God" (Rom. 8:21). Then may we eat black pudding whenever and wherever we want to! But not yet.

For now, as Martin Luther wrote, "A Christian man is the most free lord of all, and subject to none; a Christian man is the most dutiful servant of all, and subject to every one."[41]

As it was with the Master, so it is with the servant.

# 38

# The Power
# of the Tongue

I n the family in which I was brought up—like most families—there were unwritten laws against certain actions. Especially forbidden was the ultimate expression of rudeness: to stick out one's tongue at somebody.

Curiously enough, the family physician was allowed to say, "Stick out your tongue." Thus, an activity can be set in the context either of hurting or healing.

This, of course, is a point made so searchingly in the letter of James, whose teaching often distills the essence of Old Testament wisdom. The tongue, James saw, has significance out of all proportion to its size. It is like the small rudder that steers a mighty sailing vessel through the seas (James 3:4).

## Tongue and Heart

Our use of the tongue is a sure evidence of the condition of our heart. It is the hinge on which the doors into our souls swing open in order to reveal our spirits. In effect, as our words leave our mouths they are like so many media people rushing to file their reports on the condition of our souls.

Alas, the reports often seem to be contradictory: "With the tongue we praise our Lord and Father, and with it we curse men, who have been made in God's likeness" (James 3:9, NIV). The tongue can bring us into danger from the fire of hell, says Jesus (Matt. 5:22). We use it to call our brother (made in God's image) a fool. We stab his reputation in the back. Yet within a matter of hours, even minutes, we may have on the same lips the praises of God, in whose image our brother is made. The tongue unveils the deep and often unruly inconsistencies of our hearts.

We may try to mask our true spiritual condition by using the vocabulary, grammar, and syntax of grace. Yet we cannot disguise the truth, for our tongues eventually will speak the messages of our hearts. There is no long-term hiding behind the tongue. The truth will out!

Happily, that principle is two-sided. Our words may be poor and inadequate. But the tongue expresses the heart as well as the mind, the soul's ability to love as well as the brain's ability to communicate. As someone wrote to Robert Murray McCheyne in a letter that lay unopened on the day of his death: "It was not so much what you said *as your manner of speaking*."[42] The issue here is more than the ability to employ the right words. It is the revelation of the heart.

## The Tongue and Spiritual Maturity

Increased ability to control and use the tongue is an evidence of developing spiritual maturity. Of course, it is true that "even a fool is thought wise if he keeps silent, and discerning if he holds his tongue" (Prov. 17:28, NIV). But the fool's short-term self-serving is not what James has in view when he speaks about controlling the tongue (James 3:7–8). He means its *use* in speech as well as its *subjugation* to silence. Suppression is not the same thing as transformation, and it is always the latter that the Spirit seeks to effect (2 Cor. 3:18).

There is an important distinction here. We must not confuse a partially natural ability (being an easy talker or a good listener) with genuine spiritual maturity. It is one thing to cage the tiger, but another thing to tame and retrain it as a servant. To do this with the tongue is, indeed, self-mastery (James 3:2).

What, then, are the marks of the re-trained, matured-by-grace tongue?

There are few better catalogs to guide us here than David's soul-searching confession in Psalm 51:10–15:

> *Create in me a clean heart, O God,*
> *and renew a steadfast spirit within me. . . .*
> *Then I will teach transgressors Your ways,*
> *and sinners shall be converted to You.*
> *Deliver me from the guilt of bloodshed, O God,*
> *the God of my salvation,*
> *and my tongue will sing aloud of Your righteousness.*
> *O Lord, open my lips,*
> *and my mouth shall show forth Your praise.*

These verses are worth pondering with a view to self-examination and prayer for personal transformation. The tongue that has tasted the Lord's goodness speaks appropriately as well as sits silently. It praises as well as rebukes, comforts as well as challenges. Such a tongue reveals a heart that is a veritable department store of graces.

## The Tongue and Blessing

The gracious use of the tongue is ordinarily essential for service that brings blessing to others. This is one of the themes of Proverbs: "The mouth of the righteous is a well of life. . . . Wisdom is found on the lips of him who has understanding. . . . The tongue of the righteous is choice silver. . . . The lips of the righteous feed many" (Prov. 10:11, 13, 20–21). This is the kind of speech that Paul describes as "always full of grace" and "seasoned with salt" (Col. 4:6, NIV). It conveys to others a sense of the Christ who dwells in our hearts in all the fullness of His graces. Living in communion with Him, we are enabled by the Spirit to speak words that are "fitting" (Prov. 10:32, NIV), penetrating (Eccl. 12:11), and beneficial (Eph. 4:29).

Thus, we become more like our Lord Jesus, from whom supremely we learn these things. His speech was not loud or strident (Matt. 12:18–19;

cf. 2 Tim. 2:24). He became a good listener (Luke 2:46, NIV) and thus became a gracious speaker. That, at least, is how Isaiah saw the coming Messiah: "The Lord GOD has given Me the tongue of the learned, that I should know how to speak a word in season to him who is weary. He awakens Me morning by morning, He awakens My ear to hear as the learned" (Isa. 50:4).

For Jesus, spiritual speech began not in His own mouth but in "every word that proceeds from the mouth of God" (Matt. 4:4). In a word, the proof that God's Word feeds our souls will be heard in the words that come from our mouths.

# 39

# STRUGGLES

Ask a room full of Christians which of the apostles is the one with whom they most readily identify, and Simon Peter is likely to get a majority of votes. To be fair, the New Testament tells us comparatively little about most of the others. Nevertheless, there are Peter-characteristics in many of us: high points and low points, moments of joyful discovery of God's grace and moments when we put both feet in it, spiritually. Perhaps it is the size of Peter's struggle, or the repeated failures from which he was restored, that makes him so attractive to us.

But the *repetitiveness* of the failures is a troubling phenomenon. They were as real *after* Pentecost as they were *before*. Before Jesus' death, he rejected the idea of Jesus' crucifixion (Matt. 16:22); he refused to allow Jesus to wash his feet (John 13:8); he denied that he knew the Master (John 18:15–18, 25–27). Afterward, even in a vision-experience, Peter saw himself refusing the heavenly voice with a characteristically oxymoronic response to the Lord's command: "By no means, Lord" (Acts 10:14, ESV).

Admittedly this was a different context. Peter was called to preach the gospel to a group of Gentiles (the God-fearers in the house of Cornelius, centurion in the Italian Regiment). To a faithful Jew, that would have seemed outrageous—like eating the flesh of an unclean animal. Peter's every instinct was to refuse the Lord, just as he had done before and would, apparently, do again (see Gal. 2:11ff). What was going on in Peter's life that he could say, "No, Lord"?

At the heart of the issue lay Simon Peter's struggle to come to terms with both the cross *and* its implications. All of his moments of refusal seem to have involved an inability to grasp what the gospel really means.

## The Cross—Again

Perhaps we are so used to thinking about the infallibility of what the apostles wrote that we fail to take seriously enough the failures in the way they lived. In addition, we do not reflect much on the fact that in these failures and weaknesses they differed from one another.

For example, after Paul's conversion he never seems to have struggled with the cross in quite the same way Peter did. For all we know, that may have had something to do with the personal intimacy Peter had (and Paul did not have) with Jesus during His ministry. Perhaps the overpowering immediacy of Paul's encounter with the Crucified and Risen One settled the issue for him once and for all. Whatever the reason, the cross was something with which Peter struggled big-time, coming to terms with it only slowly. That he did so eventually is clear in his first letter (e.g., 1 Peter 4:1–2, 12–14).

We in the West have long been a race of Peters. That was certainly so at the time of the Reformation, when Martin Luther thundered against the church's *theologia gloriae* (theology of glory) and its refusal of *theologia crucis* (theology of the cross). The idea that we have come to trust in One who was rejected and crucified is hard for us. But we should not allow the way we wear crosses around our necks as ornaments (even as ornaments of piety) to anesthetize us from a sensitivity to the fact that it was a cruel instrument of public execution, no less lethal than a syringe, an electric chair, or a noose.

## Powerful Implications

The Puritan theologian John Owen used to make a helpful distinction between *the knowledge of the truth* and *the knowledge of the power of the truth*. It is relevant here. What Christian does not know that the heart of the gospel is "Jesus crucified for me"? But how much, Peter-like, do we resist the power of that truth penetrating our minds and prevent it mastering us?

Peter's struggle involved a resistance to the implications of the cross. That emerged most sadly in his denial of the Lord and his refusal of table fellowship with Gentiles (Gal. 2:11ff). But it was already present in his attempt to restrain Jesus from speaking of the cross (Matt. 16:22). It re-emerged in his embarrassment at seeing his Lord kneeling before him in a servant's garb. The implication was clear enough to him even without the Master spelling it out: those who follow Christ must carry the cross (John 13:1ff). There is a death to be died—to the world, to the old order, to self.

At first glance, it is hard to take in that a man like Peter, who had seen the effects of Pharisaic prejudice against his dear Master, could entertain similar prejudices against Gentile believers. Hard, that is, until one knows one's own heart. Apostolic calling and gifts did not render him immune from struggle with questions such as, "What will happen to my reputation if people see me eating with Gentiles?" At that point, he must have had to face a decision between maintaining his reputation or yielding to the self-denying implications of the cross. It is salutary to notice that his commitment did not waver when he was in Joppa and Caesarea, but Antioch was a more difficult test, particularly when some men appeared from "the circumcision party" (Gal. 2:12, ESV). Then Peter failed.

There is something very true to life about this. It mirrors our own lives. We accept the implications of the cross in one context, but we crumble in other situations.

But only when we have yielded to the cross do we really become free. Only death to self frees us from self; only death to the world frees us from bondage to the world. How well, and succinctly, did Samuel Rutherford write of the cross: "Those who can take that crabbed tree handsomely upon their back, and fasten it on cannily, shall find it such a burden as wings unto a bird, or sails to a ship."[43]

Eventually Peter found this to be true. As Jesus prophesied, he laid down his own life for Christ (John 21:18–19).

# 40

# PLAYING THE
# SECOND FIDDLE WELL

I sat in on an interview for a new associate minister. The interviewee was a widely experienced and well-proven man whom I had known for many years. As the discussion proceeded, one of our senior elders asked this question: "How well do you think you will be able to play second fiddle?"

Several thoughts passed through my mind.

The first was this little ditty:

*It takes more grace than I can tell*
*To play the second fiddle well.*

The second was that the person we were interviewing manifestly had the grace to do it.

The third was really a variation of the second: "I think this man has the Barnabas spirit. That's why we need him so much."

## *The Barnabas Spirit*

Barnabas. The name means "son of encouragement." It was not the name on his birth certificate. There he was known as Joseph Levi, originally from Cyprus (Acts 4:36). He was a man of means. He had sold a field and given the proceeds to the apostles in order to bring blessing to his fellow believers (4:37). Not only did he yield up the right to his possession of it, he yielded up his right to a say in how the proceeds would be used (the first can be present without the second!). That was the kind of man he was. He was driven by a gospel-centered desire to help, to provide for, and to edify his fellow saints. He had what the hymn describes as a "heart at leisure from itself, to soothe and sympathize."[44]

This was the man who, when the Jerusalem church gave Saul the cold shoulder, became a son of encouragement to him, took him under his wing, and nurtured him until he had found his feet and his life's work in the apostolic church (Acts 9:27).

In a life in which (among other things) Satan hindered him, Jews opposed him, Alexander the coppersmith harmed him, and Demas deserted him, Paul must have thanked God often for Joseph the Encourager. Indeed, even in days when their relationship was strained on account of John Mark, it was typical of Barnabas that he was committed (rightly or wrongly) to doing everything he could to encourage Mark and redeem his missionary career (see Acts 15:36–41). Moreover, he seems to have succeeded (see 2 Tim. 4:11).

It is impossible to read about this man without thinking that every church needs a Barnabas. Certainly every minister needs at least one Barnabas. Where can we find them?

But there is an even more basic desire we need to have: to *be* a Barnabas! Being an encourager is an essential part of genuine Christian ministry, whatever our particular gift may be (see Rom. 12:8; 1 Thess. 4:18; 5:11; Heb. 3:13; 10:25).

What are the prerequisites?

## *Playing Second Fiddle*

The first is just this: being willing to play the second fiddle well. All genuine encouragement means being willing to "consider others better than yourselves" (Phil. 2:3, NIV). That does not mean believing that you are the worst in the world at everything. That would be unreality. It means caring for others in a way that shows you put their needs before your own.

An inability to encourage someone else is usually rooted in an absorption with self that is blind to the needs or gifts of others, or a pride that cannot bring itself to praise God's grace in them. It is interesting, in this connection, to observe that the Barnabas-quality was also present in Paul's later "second fiddle," Timothy: "I have no one else like him, who takes a genuine interest in your welfare." How sad that Paul adds "everyone looks out for his own interests, not those of Jesus Christ" (Phil. 2:20–21, NIV).

Is one of the reasons for the failure of some Christian leaders simply that they themselves have never been led? Is it that they have never humbled themselves under another's leadership? Could it be that they do not know what grief their own unhumbled leadership is bringing to others?

## Spiritual Discernment

The second prerequisite is an ability to assess our fellow Christians by a truly spiritual canon of judgment. How sad to be part of a discussion in which the name of a Christian is mentioned and to hear his or her reputation stabbed in the back by the words of others! Most of us have all-too-painful contact with people who see their chief ministry as tearing fellow believers down to size. By contrast, at the end of an hour in the company of Barnabas, most of us would be able to leave feeling taller and more able to press on in serving the Lord.

What helps us here is recognizing that a person's spiritual growth cannot be measured by an assessment of his or her present height. That tells you how tall the person is, not how much he or she has grown. There is a difference. Spiritual growth is measured by the distance between where a person was and where that person now is. By that measure, someone whose understanding is less than perfect, whose character still has rough edges, or who still stumbles and falls may have traveled farther and overcome many more obstacles than his or her fellows. Looking at other Christians in this light will help us to encourage them for things we never would have noticed before.

Presumably Barnabas saw something in Saul that others failed to see. For all we know, Saul was still not the easiest of men. But even without the vision that Ananias received (Acts 9:10ff), Barnabas had eyes to see that Saul's growth in such a short time was evidence of the powerful working of God's grace.

### *Seeing Jesus Properly*

The third prerequisite is a fully biblical view of Jesus.

Yes, Jesus could pull people up short when necessary. Pharisees, hypocrites, and temple moneychangers could all feel the lash of His holy tongue. But Jesus was the supreme Son of Encouragement. A bruised reed He would not break, a smoldering wick He would not snuff out (Isa. 42:3). As an encourager, He refused to be discouraged (literally, *bruised*, Isa. 42:4). Like so many other things about being a Christian, the secret here is having a clear understanding of who Jesus is, what He is like, and what ministry He exercises, then becoming more like Him on a daily basis in all of our relationships.

Perhaps it was from long friendship with and observation of Barnabas that Paul learned to say: "From now on we regard no one from a worldly point of view. Though we once regarded Christ in this way, we do so no longer" (2 Cor. 5:16, NIV).

# CONTENTMENT: FIVE EASY STEPS?

I spoke with a close friend who had gone through a period marked by personal disappointments, discouragements, unfair treatment, and even false rumors about his character and Christian service. I was moved and impressed by his response: "My great consolation is simply this," he said, "'Godliness with contentment is great gain' (1 Tim. 6:6)."

This is truly a Christian reaction to adversity (which is the context in which spiritual contentment is most deeply tested, as well as best manifested).

Such contentment is never the result of the momentary decision of the will. It cannot be produced merely by having a well-ordered and thought-through time- and life-management plan calculated to guard us against unexpected twists of divine providence. No, true contentment means embracing the Lord's will in every aspect of His providence simply because it is *His* providence. It involves what we are in our very being, not just what we do and can accomplish.

## *Doing and Being*

Contentment is an undervalued grace. As in the seventeenth century, when Jeremiah Burroughs wrote his great work on this theme, so today it remains *The Rare Jewel of Christian Contentment.*[45] If it could be produced by programmed means ("Five steps to contentment in a month"), it would be commonplace. Instead, Christians must discover contentment the old-fashioned way: we must learn it.

Thus, we cannot "do" contentment. It is taught by God. We need to be schooled in it. It is part of the process of being transformed through the renewing of our minds (Rom. 12:1–2). It is commanded of us, but, paradoxically, it is created in us, not done by us. It is not the product of a series of actions, but of a renewed and transformed character. It involves the growth of a good tree that produces good fruit.

This seems to be a difficult principle for Christians today to grasp. Clear directives for Christian living are essential for us. But, sadly, much of the heavily programmatic teaching current in evangelicalism places such a premium on external doing and achieving that character development is set at a discount. We live in the most pragmatic society on earth (if anyone can "do it," we can). It is painful to pride to discover that the Christian life is not rooted in what we can do, but in what we need done to us.

## Knowing First

Years ago, I had a somewhat painful encounter with this "tell us and we'll do it" mentality. Halfway through a Christian students' conference where I was speaking on the assigned theme "Knowing Christ," I was summoned to meet with a deputation of staff members who seemed to feel duty-bound to confront me with the inadequacies of my first two expositions of Scripture.

"You have addressed us for two hours," they complained, "and yet, *you have not told us one single thing to do.*"

Impatience to be doing hid impatience with the apostolic principle that it is only in knowing Christ that we can do anything (cf. Phil. 3:10; 4:13)—or so it seemed to me at the time.

How does all this apply to contentment?

Christian contentment means that my satisfaction is independent of my circumstances. When Paul speaks about his own contentment in Philippians 4:11, he uses a term commonplace among the ancient Greek philosophical schools of the Stoics and Cynics. In their vocabulary, contentment meant self-sufficiency, in the sense of independence from changing circumstances.

But for Paul, contentment was rooted not in self-sufficiency but in Christ's sufficiency (Phil. 4:13). Paul said that he could do all things—both being abased and abounding—*in Christ.*

Don't skip over that last phrase. This kind of contentment is the fruit of an ongoing, intimate, deeply developed relationship with Him.

To use Paul's terms, contentment is something we have to *learn.* And here is the crux of the matter: to learn it, we must enroll in the divine school in which we are instructed by biblical teaching and providential experience.

A good sampler of the lessons learned in this school is found in Psalm 131.

## A Biblical Example

In Psalm 131, the psalmist gives us a vivid description of what it means to learn contentment. He portrays his experience in terms of a child being weaned from a milk diet onto solid food:

> LORD, *my heart is not haughty,*
> *nor my eyes lofty.*
> *Neither do I concern myself with great matters,*
> *Nor with things too profound for me.*
> *Surely I have calmed and quieted my soul,*
> *like a weaned child with his mother;*
> *like a weaned child is my soul within me.*
> *O Israel, hope in the* LORD
> *from this time forth and forever.*

To picture the scene and hear the sounds best, you need to remember that in Old Testament times weaning sometimes did not take place until a child was 3 or even 4 years old! It is hard enough for a mother to cope with an infant's dissatisfied cries, the refusal of solid food, and the struggle of wills during the weaning process. Imagine battling with a 4-year-old! That was the measure of the struggle David went through before he learned contentment.

But what was the struggle all about? David helps us by suggesting the two great issues that needed to be settled in his life.

## *Holy Ambition*

"LORD, my heart is not haughty, nor my eyes lofty" (Ps. 131:1). Ambition in and of itself is not necessarily wrong. David had been set apart for the throne, after all (1 Sam. 16:12–13). But he had a higher ambition: to trust God's wise providing, placing, and timing.

There had been occasions when David could have seized position and power by means that would have compromised his commitment to the Lord. First, Saul came into the very cave where David and his men were hiding (1 Sam. 24:3ff). Later, David and Abishai crept into Saul's tent and found him asleep (1 Sam. 26:7ff). On either occasion, he so easily could have captured or even killed Saul—who had become his enemy. After all, was he not the anointed future king? But David was content to live by the directives of God's Word and to wait patiently for God's time.

Christian contentment, therefore, is the direct fruit of having no higher ambition than to belong to the Lord and to be totally at His disposal in the place He appoints, at the time He chooses, with the provision He is pleased to make.

It was with mature wisdom, then, that the young Robert Murray McCheyne wrote, "It has always been my aim, and it is my prayer, to have no plans with regard to myself."[46] "How unusual!" we say. Yes, but what people noticed about McCheyne was how content he was to pursue one driving ambition: to know Christ (Phil. 3:10). It is not accidental that when we make Christ our ambition we discover that He becomes our sufficiency and we learn contentment in all circumstances.

## *False Preoccupations*

"Neither do I concern myself with great matters . . . things too profound for me" (Ps. 131:1). Contentment is the fruit of a mindset that understands its limitations.

David did not allow himself to be preoccupied with what God was not pleased to give to him. Neither did he allow his mind to become fixated on things God had not been pleased to explain to him.

Such preoccupations suffocate contentment. If I insist on knowing exactly what God is doing and what He plans to do with my future, if I demand to understand His ways with me in the past, I can never be content until I am equal with God. How slow we are to recognize in these subtle mental temptations the echoes of the serpent of Eden: "Express your dissatisfaction with God's ways, God's words, God's provision. Take what He has forbidden. He does not really love you, so take it! And take it now while you have the chance!"

In our Augustinian tradition, it has often been said that the first sin was *superbia*, pride. But it was more complex than that; it included discontentment. A discontented spirit is both the fruit and the evidence of an ungodly heart.

Keep these principles in view and you will not easily be caught up in a this-worldly vortex of discontentment. Go back to the school in which you will make progress in being a Christian. Study your lessons, settle the issue of ambition, make Christ your preoccupation—and you will learn to enjoy the privileges of being truly content.

PART VI

# Faithful
# to the End

*The Psalmist asked, "How shall we sing the Lord's song in a foreign land?" (Ps. 137:4). To those who do, Jesus says, "Well done, good and faithful servant" (Matt. 25:21). But how can we go on living faithfully for Christ in a faithless world?*

# 42

# The Elect Deceived?

In Matthew 24:24, Jesus warns His disciples, "False Christs and false prophets will rise and show great signs and wonders to deceive, if possible, even the elect."

These words appear to refer to the events surrounding Jerusalem's destruction in AD 70. But the deception Jesus has in view is part of an ongoing pattern. From the beginning, Satan has been deceiving God's people (Gen. 3:13). He will continue to do so until the lawless one is revealed "with all power, signs, and lying wonders" (2 Thess. 2:9–10). John's vision of the millennium ends with a worldwide rampage of deception on Satan's part (Rev. 20:8). Jesus' warning is therefore relevant to us.

## Missing the Point

"Fortunately," we may say to ourselves, "the elect are in no danger. For Jesus' words imply that we are incapable of falling prey to Satanic deception." But to read the text in this way is to miss the point, for two reasons:

*It fails to take account of the evidence of history.* Christians have been, and are, capable of being deceived. Have none of the elect been deceived in recent years into supporting "ministries" that have proved so tragically different in reality from what they professed to be? Sadly, we are more easily addicted to the spectacular ("signs and wonders") than to the substantial, to novelty ("false prophets") than to a wholesome orthodoxy. If we think Christians cannot be deceived, the deception has already begun.

195

*It misunderstands the nature of the impossibility.* Jesus did not say the elect were incapable of being deceived. We are all only too capable of it. Nevertheless, we are given this assurance: God will protect and preserve His people. Like Simon Peter, they will be shielded by the prayers of Christ and the power of God (Luke 22:31–32). This is accomplished through the activity of faith (1 Peter 1:5).

## Guarded

But how can we guard ourselves against spiritual deception?

By developing *sensitivity*, we become aware of Satan's strategies in our lives (2 Cor. 2:11).

*Have you learned what they are?*

By developing *self-knowledge*, we recognize how weak we are. Since nothing good dwells in our flesh (Rom. 7:18), we need constantly to depend on the Lord.

*Do you?*

By developing *an appetite for God's Word*, we are "trained by constant practice to distinguish good from evil" (Heb. 5:14, ESV), and we grow in discernment.

*Is that true of you today?*

# 43

# Naming the Enemy

I n his remarkable little book *Towards Spiritual Maturity*, William Still[47] describes what he calls "the three dimensions of the cross." Christ, he writes, deals with sin as power, with sins as deeds that bring guilt, and with Satan as the Christian's enemy. I often used to hear him talk about "the Root" (sin), "the Fruit" (sins), and "the Brute" (the Devil).

## *The Third Dimension*

That third dimension is important. We tend either to ignore or to exaggerate the activity of the Devil. Preaching and counseling, for example, do not always reflect the New Testament's teaching that our fundamental struggle is "against the spiritual forces of evil" (Eph. 6:12, ESV). On the other hand, too many Christians confuse sickness and sin with demon-possession. How Devil-like to push us to one extreme or the other!

In the New Testament, the spiritual enemy is portrayed in various ways. For instance, he is called a liar (John 8:44) and the hinderer of God's work (1 Thess. 2:18). But one of the most graphic biblical portrayals of him is in the vision of his overthrow in Revelation 12–13. Here John sees him as the serpent of the Garden of Eden who has devoured so many creatures that he has now grown into a mighty dragon (Rev. 12:9). He helps us to recognize the enemy's strategy by giving him titles: deceiver, Devil, Satan, accuser. He is all four, in the most literal sense with a vengeance.

## The Deceiver

By the use of his agents, the Evil One "deceives those who dwell on the earth" (Rev. 13:13–14). He looks like a lamb, but his voice is that of a dragon (13:11)!

From the beginning, this has been his activity. "The serpent deceived me, and I ate," confessed Eve (Gen. 3:13; cf. 1 Tim. 2:14). As the god of this age, he blinds minds (2 Cor. 4:4). We experience that whenever we fall into sin: temptation fills our horizon and we lose sight of what lies beyond it; we stop thinking clearly. Later, in our grief, we say, "If only I had seen the consequences." But we were deceived and blinded.

What is the safeguard? Remember how Jesus defended Himself when the enemy tried to deceive Him in the wilderness temptations? Our Lord had hidden God's Word in His heart; He was able to think biblically, that is, *clearly*. He saw through the deception.

## The Devil

This name (from a compound of the Greek verb *to throw*) conveys the idea of slandering, of throwing falsehoods against someone; "mudslinging," we might say.

But on whom does the Devil sling his mud? On God, first of all.

The Evil One began to do this in the Garden of Eden. Adam and Eve were surrounded by an abundance of good things: the creation, the animals, the rivers, the trees, the flowers, the fruit! But the serpent said, "God has put you here to mock you. Did He say, 'You must not eat from any of these trees'?" (see Gen. 3:3). God had done no such thing. He had given them everything to enjoy (Gen. 2:16). Only one tree was forbidden (2:17).

Do you see the Devil's slander? He was attacking God's loving, generous character and accusing Him of being a cynical Creator. It is one of His favorite strategies. "Look at your circumstances," he whispers, seeking to disguise his dragon-voice, "God doesn't really love you!" We should not be "ignorant of his devices" (2 Cor. 2:11).

What is our defense? Here is Paul's: "God demonstrates His own love toward us, in that while we were still sinners, Christ died for us" (Rom. 5:8). Let the cross silence the Devil's slanders and convince you of the wonder of God's love.

## Satan

Some commentators suggest that the root idea here includes attacking someone from an ambush. The attack is unexpected and the attacker is hidden.

Think of Job. The tension created by reading the book of Job lies in the fact that we—the audience—know something that is hidden from Job himself. We know that these sufferings, while under the sovereign hand of God, are caused by Satan. But Satan is hidden from Job. He has no idea that Satan is behind his suffering. He has been ambushed.

In another connection, think of Jesus when His dear friend Peter took hold of Him to restrain Him from going to the cross. But the Lord identified the real source of the attack, saying, in essence: "Out of my sight, *Satan*" (see Mark 8:33). While His physical eyes saw only Simon, His spiritual sight detected and exposed Satan.

Thankfully, God protects us from Satan even at times when we are not aware of His protection. But how can we develop Jesus-like discernment? By Spirit-aided digestion of the solid food of God's wisdom. Thus we are "trained . . . to distinguish good from evil" (Heb. 5:14, ESV).

## The Accuser of the Brothers

The Enemy keeps a diary of our guilt and failure. In God's courtroom, he accuses us (cf. Zech. 3:1–2); in the courtroom of our own consciences, we hear the echoes. John Newton knew about this. At times he felt himself to be:

> *Bowed down beneath a load of sin,*
> *By Satan sorely pressed.*[48]

How can we conquer Satan when he whispers that we are not fit to be Christians? John saw how the saints accomplish this: "They overcame him by the blood of the Lamb and by the word of their testimony" (Rev. 12:11).

What is this testimony? It is this: "Who shall bring a charge against God's elect? It is God who justifies. Who is he who condemns? It is Christ who died, and furthermore is also risen, who is even at the right hand of God, who also makes intercession for us" (Rom. 8:33–34). So we can sing with Newton:

*Be thou my shield and hiding place*
*That, sheltered near thy side,*
*I may my fierce accuser face,*
*And tell him thou hast died.*[49]

It is always a first principle of warfare that we get to know the strength and tactics of our enemy, as well as our own resources. That is just as true of spiritual conflict as it is of military combat!

# 44

# GROWING STRONG IN THE WAR ZONE

How easily the words "We need to get back to the early church" flow from our lips. Perhaps there is something innate in us that wants to look back to the imagined golden days of the past, when giants walked the land. Oh, to have been in John Calvin's Geneva, John Knox's Edinburgh, John Owen's London, Jonathan Edwards' Northampton, and, above all, Jerusalem in the days of the apostles!

But we need only to read the sermons of the men mentioned above to realize that distance has lent a deceiving enchantment to the view. Calvin's Genevans could be an unruly lot, Knox's earlier enthusiasts waxed cold, Owen could complain about the ignorance and lethargy of the church, and Edwards' people removed him from his Northampton pulpit in which he had preached some of the most remarkable sermons ever heard in North America.

We should have learned from the early church that this is how it is. Whether in days of revival or of mediocrity, it is always at the cost of blood, sweat, and tears that the church is built. Indeed, when Jesus first spoke about church building in Matthew 16:18, He made it clear that it takes place in a war zone. He spoke of conflict with the gates of hell: "And I also say to you that you are Peter, and on this rock I will build My church, and the gates of Hades shall not prevail against it."

The first church in Jerusalem experienced sudden, exponential growth.

This is an underlying theme of the opening chapters of the book of Acts: three thousand were added on the Day of Pentecost (2:41); daily conversions followed (2:47); an increase to five thousand men plus families soon came (4:4); more were added constantly (5:14); and large numbers of priests believed (6:7). But simultaneously, the apostle-pastors were faced with deep and sometimes sinister opposition.

## Suffering: A Mark of the Church?

The most obvious way in which this surfaced presents us with a paradox: even as the church grew, it faced constant persecution. Acts 2, 4, 5, 6, and 7 are all punctuated by accounts of derision, opposition, suffering, and persecution.

Strangely, the confessional formulations of the marks and notes of the church (one, holy, catholic, and apostolic; preaching, sacraments, and discipline) make no mention of suffering. Perhaps our forefathers were so used to it that they simply assumed its presence. But it is not possible to read through the New Testament without realizing that suffering and persecution are perennial marks of the Lord's people. Those who responded to the gospel in repentance and faith suffered as a result.

It was no part of Luke's purpose in writing Acts to explain in detail how the apostles ministered in such a context. But we get a glimpse of the kind of pastoral instruction they must have given in Peter's first letter. Suffering, he underlined, is a basic element in the structure of the Christian life (1 Peter 4:12).

Faith is tested and proved genuine through trials (1 Peter 1:6–7). Like gold refined in a furnace, trials can cleanse and purify the Christian. The persecution that is intended to destroy you actually has the opposite effect—it makes you rely more on Christ and draws you to live closer to Him. The person who suffers in the flesh for Christ is the person who rejects the enticements of sin (1 Peter 4:1–2). When you have faced up to the cost of discipleship—socially, materially, even physically—a new decisiveness enters into your lifestyle.

Suffering also provides the theater in which Christians demonstrate—by the radically different way they respond to opposition—that they belong to a counterculture or, better, to a Jesus culture. They submit to government, not for its own sake but for the Lord's (1 Peter 2:13). They submit even to harsh taskmasters because they want to follow in the steps of Christ, who left an example (1 Peter 2:18–21).

The word "example" here (*hupogrammos*) is very evocative. It was used of the copper-plate handwriting of the teacher that was to be imitated by the pupil. Jesus has written out the vocabulary of Christian living for us; we are to copy it on the pages of the autobiography we are writing. Some words are not easy to learn—especially these ones: p-e-r-s-e-c-u-t-i-o-n and s-u-f-f-e-r-i-n-g. But they are key words if the name of Jesus is to be legible in our lives.

## Suffering and Glory

In God's workshop in this world, suffering is the raw material out of which glory is forged (1 Peter 1:7; 4:12–13). That is standard New Testament teaching. But there is a subtle development of it in Peter: "If you are reproached for the name of Christ, blessed are you, *for the Spirit of glory and of God rests upon you*" (1 Peter 4:14, emphasis added).

The prospect of future glory has been a great consolation to believers throughout the ages. But Peter is saying more than that. Glory belongs not only to the "there and then"; it is part of the "here and now" of suffering. The Spirit who uses our sufferings to produce glory gives advance indications of the final product in the present lives of believers.

We get a glimpse of that sometimes in older Christians who have seen trials; we see that there is a grace in them that eludes definition. It is etched into their lives from beyond. A touch of the glory of the future world seems already to clothe them in the present one.

Peter's bottom line is this: don't be surprised by suffering (1 Peter 4:12).

But how can twenty-first-century Christians in the Western world be un-surprised in times of suffering? We can do so only by being delivered from a faulty understanding of what it means to be a Christian. Jesus was crucified by this world. To become a Christian by definition means to follow a cross-bearing Savior and Lord. It means to be identified with Him in such a way that opposition to Him will inevitably touch us.

Paul said that he bore on his body the marks of Jesus (Gal. 6:17). So perhaps we should ask:

*Hast thou no scar?*
*No hidden scar on foot, or side, or hand?*
*I hear thee sung as mighty in the land;*
*I hear them hail thy bright, ascendant star.*
*Hast thou no scar?*

*Hast thou no wound?*
*Yet, I was wounded by the archers, spent.*
*Leaned Me against the tree to die, and rent*
*By ravening beasts that compassed Me, I swooned:*
*Hast thou no wound?*

*No wound? No scar?*
*Yet as the Master shall the servant be,*
*And pierced are the feet that follow Me.*
*But thine are whole. Can he have followed far*
*Who hast no wound or scar?*[50]

Are you a marked man or woman?

# 45

# GUESS WHO
# IS OUT OF JAIL

Here is a piece of Bible trivia: Can you identify the only member of the New Testament church whose name appears in the letter to the Hebrews?

Here are five clues:

*Clue No. 1*: This person seems to have been known to the author.

That is not much help in narrowing down the field.

*Clue No. 2*: This person had recently been released from imprisonment.

Got him yet?

*Clue No. 3*: This person was known very well by the apostle Paul.

Still wondering?

*Clue No. 4*: This person's mother was a Jewess and his father was a Gentile.

Still not enough?

*Clue No. 5*: Paul wrote two letters to this person.

Got it now?

If you still have not worked it out, it is time to look at the third to last verse in Hebrews.

So what is the point of this piece of Bible trivia? Well, for one thing it means we know the name of one person who did *not* write Hebrews! For another, it tells us something about that person we otherwise never would have known. And, perhaps most interesting of all, it suggests that this person, a Jew by birth, raised on the Old Testament Scriptures that feature so dominantly in the letter to the Hebrews, mixed the promise of God with faith (Heb. 4:2), fixed his gaze on Jesus (Heb. 12:2–3), and endured suffering for His sake.

The answer to the question is, of course, Timothy!

Here is another interesting detail about many of the New Testament believers whose names are mentioned in the correspondence of the apostles: they frequently illustrate the very lessons the letters are seeking to teach. Timothy is no exception. Indeed, he obviously lived up to the beautiful words Paul wrote about him in Philippians: "I have no one like him. . . . You know Timothy's proven worth, how as a son with a father he has served with me in the gospel" (Phil. 2:20, 22, ESV). Yes, indeed, wrote the author of Hebrews, "our brother Timothy has been set free" (Heb. 13:23).

But what a tantalizing statement!

Where had Timothy been imprisoned? Had he made it to Rome in time to be with Paul before the apostle's execution? Had he been able to bring the cloak Paul had left with Carpus at Troas (and what does that say about how few possessions Paul must have had?), as well as Paul's precious books and parchments (2 Tim. 4:13)?

Who knows? But these enigmatic words in Hebrews tell us two important things.

### The Fruit of God's Work

First, they tell us about the rich fruit that God's Word, along with the ministry and encouragement of His people, bore in Timothy's life. Most commentators envisage Timothy as a comparatively young, possibly shy and timid person, perhaps with some stomach problems. The evidence can be overdone, of course. But certainly he was not a "gung-ho" personality. Unlike the famous Ignatius of Antioch, who seemed determined to suffer martyrdom, Timothy perhaps needed the apostle's encouragements not to be ashamed of the gospel and to take his share of suffering (2 Tim. 1:8). Perhaps he needed to be assured that this was *the* pathway for all believers (2 Tim. 3:12), but that the Lord would not desert him.

Certainly Paul's words paving the way for Timothy's arrival in Corinth—

"When Timothy comes, see that you put him at ease among you" (1 Cor. 16:10, ESV)—do not suggest that the young evangelist enjoyed dealing with controversial situations or difficult people.

Yet, Timothy had been faithful; like Moses, he counted the reproach of Christ greater wealth than the treasures of this world (Heb. 11:26). He had endured. And now he was being delivered.

What message does this hold for us? If we find Hebrews' description of the Christian way rigorous to the point of intimidating, we must remember this: "The God of peace who brought up our Lord Jesus from the dead, that great Shepherd of the sheep, through the blood of the everlasting covenant, [will] make *you* complete in every good work to do His will . . ." (Heb. 13:20–21, emphasis added).

### Character of Leaders

Second, the reference to Timothy helps to illustrate a theme that runs through Hebrews 13—the characteristics of true leaders and the attitude we are to develop and maintain with respect to them: "Remember your leaders, those who spoke to you the word of God. Consider the outcome of their way of life, and imitate their faith" (Heb. 13:7, ESV); "Obey your leaders and submit to them, for they are keeping watch over your souls, as those who will have to give an account. Let them do this with joy and not with groaning, for that would be of no advantage to you" (Heb. 13:17, ESV).

In his relationship with Paul, Timothy exemplified the disposition of a follower: he remembered him, observed the fruit of his faith, and imitated it. He submitted gladly to Paul's leadership, thankful for his spiritual father and for Paul's willingness to take spiritual responsibility for him and to mentor him. This was why—in words that Hebrews echoes (13:17)—for Paul the leader to see Timothy his disciple was to be "filled with joy" (2 Tim. 1:4).

It is thus that true leaders are generally formed and developed. When leaders have never been led—not merely at the formal level, but in the sense of a heart devotion and heart submission to wise and caring leadership—

they are not usually well-equipped to lead others. They may even expect a submission they have never been willing to experience themselves. "After all, I was destined for leadership, not discipleship!" they may foolishly, and often disastrously, think.

Because this is the calling of leaders—so beautifully illustrated in Timothy—it is also the reason the author of Hebrews can call us to "obey" and "submit" to them. Thus, their leadership will not be a burden ("not with groaning," as the ESV expressively translates it), but a joy (Heb. 13:17).

What if all leaders in the church were like you? Are you a walking version of the letter to the Hebrews?

Have you shown heart submission to the leadership of others? Are you prepared to suffer for others, to go through trials? Perhaps you are a ruling elder. When things get tough, rough, and sore, do you simply complain, or perhaps tend to pull back a little and look to the teaching elder/pastor as though to say, "The tough ones are for you to handle"?

Most of us are church members, not church leaders. Are you a joy or a burden? What a telling question! How sad when we count—of all things—argumentativeness, a domineering spirit, an angular personality, or an ongoing motif of cynicism about other believers as a grace. Have we no idea that we make our leaders groan rather than rejoice? Should we not make this one of the questions for church membership: "Will you seek to be a source of joy to your leaders?"

Timothy is a model for both disciples and leaders. He was the latter because he had learned to be the former. And once we have been both, we, too, become living letters, versions of the great letter to the Hebrews, those in whom the Lord is "working . . . what is well pleasing in His sight, through Jesus Christ, to whom be glory forever and ever. Amen" (Heb. 13:21). And amen!

# 46

# An Anatomy
# of Temptation

I t was the spring of that ever-to-be-remembered year. Usually his mind turned to new projects, and he felt eager to see his life's work expand. But for some ill-defined reason, he felt different this year. A strange mixture of restlessness, unease, and lethargy seemed to have gripped him. He needed a break; after all, he surely deserved one. There would be other years for vigorous leadership. Yet he was not satisfied; the spirit of restlessness remained.

Early one evening he lay down, briefly, on the couch; but soon he was up, puttering around. He felt enclosed. A breath of fresh air would clear his head. He made his way out to the roof garden and looked around.

You know the rest of the story:

*He saw a woman . . . very beautiful. [He] sent messengers, and took her; and . . . lay with her. . . . She returned to her house. . . . She sent . . . and said, "I am with child."* —2 SAMUEL 11:2–5

## Catalog of Intrigue

The catalog of intrigue that followed makes for chilling reading.

*Plan A:* Disguise the sin (get the husband home from the front for a quiet weekend with his wife so that the baby will be assumed to be his). *Failure:* The man has too deep a sense of the sacrifices of his comrades not to share them.

*Plan B:* Arrange for the husband to be cruelly exposed in battle and slain. *Success:* "Then the men of the city came out and fought with Joab. And some of the people of the servants of David fell; and Uriah the Hittite died also" (2 Sam. 11:17).

## True Success?

The way was now open for him to have the woman—Bathsheba was her name—all to himself. A marriage was arranged; the child was born. It would soon be spring again. But it was winter in the man's soul.

And what was the name of this adulterer, this deceiver, this man who designed the death of one of his mighty men of valor as if it were an unavoidable casualty of war? David, of course—King David.

But David was no longer the "man after [God's] own heart" he had once been (1 Sam. 13:14).

But then "the LORD sent Nathan to David" (2 Sam. 12:1). His sins were exposed; the divine judgment was pronounced. David would live, but the child would die (2 Sam. 12:13–14). David "pleaded with God for the child . . . fasted . . . lay all night on the ground" (2 Sam. 12:16). On day seven the child—David's nameless son—died.

James seems to echo this story deliberately in words that can best be described as an anatomy of temptation:

> *Each one is tempted when he is drawn away by his own desires and enticed. Then, when desire has conceived, it gives birth to sin; and sin, when it is full-grown, brings forth death.* —JAMES 1:14–15

Follow his lessons in spiritual anatomy:

**Stage 1:** *Temptation is fueled by our evil "desires."* Unlike Christ, we are not able to say that Satan can find no landing ground in our lives (John 14:30).

Unless we believe with the likes of Robert Murray McCheyne that "the seeds of all sins are in my heart, and perhaps all the more dangerously that I do not see them,"[51] we are unlikely to watch and pray lest we enter into temptation (Matt. 26:41).

**First Antidote:** Know your own heart, and guard it.

**Stage 2:** *Temptation progresses by both negative and positive means.* Its strategy involves a twofold movement: "lure," then "entice." First comes the loosening of our secure moorings; then, when we are drifting, we become caught up in the strong currents of the fleeting, but all-too-appealing, "pleasures of sin" (Heb. 11:25).

We see both in David. He was "lured" from his royal duties to God and to his people (a fact all-too-painfully underlined by Uriah's contrasting faithfulness; see 2 Sam. 11:6–17). He became adrift in a sea of temptation without anchor or rudder. Then David was "enticed." The sight of Bathsheba's beauty, and sadly perhaps her willingness or at least weakness, was itself adequate to destroy his already depleted defenses.

Temptation does not always occur in this dramatic fashion. But its basic pattern is usually the same.

**Second Antidote:** Know your Christian duties, and stick to them.

**Stage 3:** *Temptation conquers when unguarded inclinations meet opportunity.* Sometimes when we have strong sinful desires we lack the external opportunity to satisfy them. At other times, opportunities arise when our desires have been diverted to other pursuits. But we would be naive to confuse these situations with an ability to resist temptation at its full height. Then we need to be able to wield the Spirit's sword.

David's escape route could not have been clearer. The directions were written on his palace walls: "You shall not covet . . . your neighbor's wife"; "You shall not steal"; "You shall not commit adultery"; "You shall not bear false witness"; "You shall not murder" (Ex. 20:13–17). But if he saw them, he was blind to their importance. Bathsheba was so near that she obscured all heavenly wisdom from his vision.

**Third Antidote:** When inclinations to sin encounter opportunities, remember and keep the commandments. "Great peace have those who love Your law, and nothing causes them to stumble" (Ps. 119:165).

**Stage 4:** *Temptation unresisted leads to death.* The death of David's son illustrates the final fruit of sin. Its wages are death (Rom. 6:23)—death as the destruction of blessing, death as separation from God, death as decay, loss, and darkness. If only David had asked, "Where will these desires lead me?" But when our desires bring their objects near, vision is obscured. We forget Scripture's sobering warnings that we reap what we sow, that the mind set on the flesh is death, that only those who put to death the misdeeds of the flesh can live (Gal. 6:7–8; Rom. 8:6, 13).

**Fourth Antidote:** Always ask where an action will lead you, and what its final destination will be, before you become volitionally or affectionally drawn into it. Live always for the future, and in such a way that you will not be ashamed at Christ's coming.

Yes, we fail. But here is a word of encouragement from one who likewise failed: "Brothers . . . if you do these things, you will never fall, and you will receive a rich welcome into the eternal kingdom of our Lord and Savior Jesus Christ" (2 Peter 1:10–11, NIV).

What things?

*His divine power has granted to us all things that pertain to life and god-liness, through the knowledge of him who called us to his own glory and excellence, by which he has granted to us his precious and very great prom-ises, so that through them you may become partakers of the divine nature, having escaped from the corruption that is in the world because of sinful desire. For this very reason, make every effort to supplement your faith with virtue, and virtue with knowledge, and knowledge with self-control, and self-control with steadfastness, and steadfastness with godliness, and godli-ness with brotherly affection, and brotherly affection with love. For if these qualities are yours and are increasing, they keep you from being ineffective or unfruitful in the knowledge of our Lord Jesus Christ.*

—2 Peter 1:3–8, esv

Here is the apostolic medicine for sickly souls—prescribed by one who fell grievously ill but was raised up!

# 47

# Danger: Apostasy!

t the end of a theology course I was teaching (happily, I cannot now be sure where), I included the following question in the exam:

> "Then I saw that there was a Way to Hell even from the Gates of Heaven, as well as from the City of Destruction" (John Bunyan, *The Pilgrim's Progress*). *Discuss.*

Some students, rightly realizing that a discussion of the doctrine of perseverance was probably expected, confidently affirmed that the author of this quotation was obviously an Arminian!

The experience taught me two sobering lessons:

1. There are many Christians who have never read *The Pilgrim's Progress* (Bunyan, of course, was a Calvinist!).

2. These students probably had never taken the "warning passages" in Scripture with full theological seriousness.

Such warning passages serve almost as punctuation marks in the letter to the Hebrews, written as it was to encourage Christians to keep running the race of faith and not to turn back (Heb. 12:1–2; 13:22). It is a letter that speaks quite specifically of the danger of apostasy: "Take care, brothers, lest there be in any of you an evil, unbelieving heart, leading you to fall away [*apostēnai*] from the living God" (Heb. 3:12, ESV). Other significant statements include Hebrews 2:1–4; 3:7–15; 4:1–11; 6:1–12; 10:26–39; and 12:14–29.

How are we to understand this teaching?

## God Perseveres

First, we should regard it as a settled biblical principle that God perseveres in the salvation of His chosen people. To hold any other view not only denies the doctrine of the saints' perseverance—with its corollary, the eternal security of believers—it evacuates several major biblical doctrines of their significance.

These doctrines include election, predestination, and the ongoing work of the Spirit (Phil. 1:6 and 2:12–13 become very pale and sickly in this view). The prayers of Christ fall in pieces before the throne of God (contrary to John 17:11); His grip on His sheep is mysteriously paralyzed (contrary to John 10:27–30). Furthermore, the possibility of assurance about future salvation disappears if it is founded on uncertainty. Where then the confidence of Romans 8:28–39?

## We Also Must Persevere

Second, we need to recognize that the doctrine of perseverance means that believers themselves must *actually persevere*, often in the face of almost overwhelming pressures to give up. Perseverance is sweetened by grace, but it does not thereby become effortless. There are temptations to be faced; there is indwelling sin to be resisted; and the wiles of the Devil still have to be detected and the armor of God worn in order to overcome him. We may even have to resist to the point of shedding our blood (cf. Heb. 12:4).

*But these are exactly the characteristics of true faith.* The message of Hebrews is, therefore: make sure your faith is like this. That is the whole point of the description of the great heroes of the faith in Hebrews 11, leading up to Christ, *the* Hero of the Faith in 12:1–2.

## Grace, Not Experiences

Third, we need to realize that spiritual experiences are not identical with saving grace.

This principle underlies Hebrews 6:4–12, often thought to prove beyond a doubt that a person who is a true Christian may commit apostasy. Indeed, verses 4–6 have been described as the clearest description of a Christian in the entire New Testament: being enlightened, tasting the heavenly gift, sharing in the Spirit, and tasting the goodness of the Word of God and the powers of the coming age.

But the striking thing about the experiences these verses describe is not so much what they say as *what they omit*. Nothing is said here about trust in Christ, about repentance, about bearing the cross, or about loving the Lord Jesus Christ and our fellow believers.

In fact, these verses could have been written of Judas Iscariot. The light of Christ entered his life. He tasted the heavenly gift and shared experiences of the Spirit with the other apostles. He was exposed to the goodness of the Word of God for several years. The powers of the coming age were released all around him in Jesus' healing and saving ministry. But Judas was never made clean by Christ (John 13:10–11); he had not been chosen (13:18). Jesus knew long before His betrayal that Judas was "a devil" (John 6:70). There was no faith in him! In the end, there was no repentance, only regret (Matt. 27:3).

The author of Hebrews actually made this distinction clear to his first readers. When people who have had these spiritual experiences "fall away" (Heb. 6:6), he said, it is impossible for us to restore them. By contrast, he told his readers, "we are confident of *better things* concerning you, yes, things that *accompany salvation*" (Heb. 6:9, emphasis added). These believers had faith in the hope of the gospel and had displayed the love that is the central fruit of the Spirit. This indicates that real and lasting salvation was theirs.

## Do Not Neglect Grace

The message is clear. Do not confuse great experiences with great grace. Some have done that and made spiritual shipwreck. Rather, as the author counsels us, be on your guard against the neglect of grace (2:3); be careful that your heart is not hardened by the deceitfulness of sin (3:13); and see that you do not fall prey to disobedience (3:18; 4:6) and do not lack faith (4:3). Beware a careless attitude to the importance of fellowship (10:25); guard against sinning deliberately (10:26); do not shrink back in the face of difficulties (10:38); and do not "refuse Him who speaks" through His mighty Word (12:25).

There is a path to hell from the gates of heaven. Sadly, some have not come by the way of grace, faith, and repentance. They may have been self-deceived. That is why Hebrews sounds the note of self-examination. Make sure your profession of faith involves the possession of Christ.

No one who hears Christ's voice, listens in faith, and follows Him can ever perish (John 10:27–30). Stumble we may, but He will keep us from permanently falling (Jude 24). For we have His own promise:

*All that the Father gives Me will come to Me, and the one who comes to Me*
*I will by no means cast out.*　　　　　　　　　—JOHN 6:37

# 48

# THE PRACTICE
# OF MORTIFICATION

The aftermath of a conversation can change the way we later think of its significance.

My friend—a younger minister—sat down with me at the end of a conference in his church and said, "Before we retire tonight, just take me through the steps that are involved in helping someone mortify sin." We sat talking about this for a little longer and then went to bed; I hoped he felt as blessed as I did by our conversation.

I still wonder whether he asked his question as a pastor or simply for himself—or both.

How would you best answer his question? The first thing to do is to *turn to the Scriptures*. Yes, turn to John Owen (never a bad idea!) or to some other counselor dead or alive. But remember that we have not been left only to good human resources in this area. We need to be taught from "the mouth of God" if the principles we are learning to apply are to carry with them both the *authority* of God and the *promise* of God to make them work. Thus our Lord Jesus Himself believed (Matt. 4:4).

Several passages come to mind for study: Romans 8:13; Romans 13:8–14 (Augustine's life-transforming text); 2 Corinthians 6:14–7:1; Ephesians 4:17–5:21; Colossians 3:1–17; 1 Peter 4:1–11; 1 John 2:28–3:11. Significantly, only two of these passages contain the verb *mortify* ("put to death"). Equally significantly, the context of each of these passages is broader than the single exhortation to put sin to death. As we shall see, this observation turns out to be of considerable importance.

## A Good Starting Place

Colossians 3:1–17 is probably the best place for us to begin.

The believers in Colossae were relatively young Christians. Theirs had been a radical experience of conversion to Christ from paganism. They had entered a gloriously new and liberating world of grace. In fact, perhaps—if we may read between the lines—they had felt for a while as if they had been delivered not only from sin's penalty but even from its influence, so marvelous was their new freedom. But then, of course, sin reared its ugly head again. Having experienced the "already" of grace, they were discovering the painful "not yet" of ongoing sanctification. Sound familiar? Just at this point keen young Christians can be all too vulnerable to "quick fixes."

But as in our evangelical subculture, quick fixes do not solve long-term problems. Unless the Colossians gained a firm grasp of gospel principles, they were at risk of falling prey to false teachers with promises of a higher spiritual life. That was what Paul feared (Col. 2:8, 16). Holiness-producing methods were in vogue (Col. 2:21–22). Moreover, they *seemed* to be deeply spiritual, just the thing for earnest young believers. But, in fact, says Paul, such things "are of no value against the indulgence of the flesh" (Col. 2:23).

Not new methods, but only an understanding of how the gospel method works, can provide an adequate foundation and pattern for dealing with sin. This is the theme of Colossians 3:1–17.

Paul gives us the pattern and rhythm we need. Like Olympic long jumpers, we will not succeed unless we go back from the *point of action* to a point from which we can *gain energy* for the strenuous effort of dealing with sin.

How, then, does Paul teach us to do this?

## New Identity

First of all, Paul underlines how important it is for us *to be familiar with our new identity in Christ* (3:1–4).

How often, when we fail spiritually, we lament that we forgot who we really were.

Christians have a new identity. We are no longer "in Adam" but "in Christ"; no longer in the flesh but in the Spirit; no longer dominated by the old creation but living in the new (Rom. 5:12–21; 8:9; 2 Cor. 5:17).

Paul takes time to expound this:

- We have died with Christ (3:3; we have even been buried with Him, 2:12).
- We have been raised with Christ (3:1).
- Our true life is hidden with Christ in God (3:3).
- We are so inseparably united to Christ that we will appear in glory with Him (3:4).

Failure to deal with the presence of sin can often be traced back to spiritual amnesia—forgetting our new, true, real identity. As a believer, I am someone who has been delivered from the dominion of sin and who therefore is free and motivated to fight against the remnants of sin in my heart. You must know, rest in, think through, and act upon your new identity—you are in Christ.

## Sin Exposed

Second, Paul goes on to expose *the workings of sin in every area of our lives* (Col. 3:5–11). If we are to deal with sin biblically, we must not make the mistake of thinking that we can limit our attack to only one area of failure. All sin must be dealt with. Thus, Paul ranges through the manifestation of sin in private life (v. 5), everyday public life (v. 8), and church life (vv. 9–11; "one another" and "here" indicate the church fellowship).

The challenge in mortification is akin to the challenge in dieting (itself a form of mortification!). Once we begin, we discover that there are all kinds of reasons we are overweight. We are really dealing with ourselves, not simply with calories. I am the problem, not the potato chips! Mortifying sin is a whole-of-life change.

## *Practical Guidelines*

Third, Paul's exposition provides us with *practical guidance for mortifying sin.*

Sometimes it seems as if Paul gives exhortations ("Put to death . . . ," 3:5) without giving "practical" help to answer our "how-to" questions. Often today Christians go to Paul to tell them *what* to do and then to the local Christian bookstore to discover *how* to do it!

Why this bifurcation? Probably because we do not linger long enough over what Paul is saying. We do not sink our thinking deeply into the Scriptures. For, characteristically, whenever Paul issues an exhortation, he surrounds it with hints as to how we are to put it into practice.

This is certainly true here. Notice how this passage helps to answer our "how-to" questions.

1. *Learn to admit sin for what it really is.* Call a spade a spade—call it "fornication" (v. 5), not "I'm being tempted a little"; call it "uncleanness" (v. 5), not "I'm struggling with my thought life"; call it "covetousness, which is idolatry" (v. 5), not "I think I need to order my priorities a bit better." This pattern runs right through the whole section. How powerfully it unmasks self-deception—and helps us to unmask sin lurking in the hidden corners of our hearts!

2. *See sin for what it really is in God's presence.* "Because of these the wrath of God is coming" (3:6). The masters of the spiritual life spoke of dragging our lusts to the cross (kick and scream, though they will), to a wrath-bearing Christ. My sin leads not to lasting pleasure but to holy divine displeasure. See the true nature of your sin in the light of its punishment. Too easily we think that sin is less serious in Christians than it is in unbelievers: "It's forgiven, isn't it?" Not if we continue in it (1 John 3:9)! Take a heaven's-eye view of sin and feel the shame of that in which you once walked (3:7; cf. Rom. 6:21).

3. *Recognize the inconsistency of your sin.* You have put off the "old man," and have put on the "new man" (3:9–10). You are no longer your "old self." The identity you had "in Adam" is gone. The "old man was crucified

with Him [Christ], that the body of sin [probably meaning "life in the body dominated by sin"] might be done away with, that we should no longer be slaves of sin" (Rom. 6:6). New people live new lives. Anything less than this is a contradiction of who we are "in Christ."

4. *Put sin to death (v. 5)*. It is as "simple" as that. Refuse it, starve it, and reject it. You cannot "mortify" sin without the pain of the kill. There is no other way!

But notice that Paul sets this in a very important broader context. The *negative* task of putting sin to death will not be accomplished in isolation from the *positive* call of the gospel to "put on" the Lord Jesus Christ (Rom. 13:14).

Paul spells this out in Colossians 3:12–17. Sweeping the house clean simply leaves us open to a further invasion of sin. But when we understand the "glorious exchange" principle of the gospel of grace, then we begin to make some real advances in holiness. Sinful desires and habits not only must be *rejected* but *exchanged* for Christ-like graces (3:12) and actions (3:13). As we are clothed in Christ's character and His graces are held together by love (v.14), not only in our private lives but also in the church fellowship (vv. 12–16), Christ's name and glory will be manifested and exalted in and among us (3:17).

These are some of the things my friend and I talked about that memorable Sunday evening.

We did not have an opportunity later to ask each other "How are you doing?" It was the last conversation we had together. He died some months later.

I have often wondered how the months in between went in his life. But the earnest personal and pastoral concern in his question still echoes in my mind. Our last conversation has for me a similar effect to the one Charles Simeon said he felt from the eyes of his much-loved portrait of the great Henry Martyn: "Don't trifle!"[52]

# 49

# EXPELLING WORLDLINESS
# WITH A NEW AFFECTION

The remarkable Thomas Chalmers (1780–1847) was one of the most gifted men of his time—a mathematician, an evangelical theologian, an economist, and an ecclesiastical, political, and social reformer all in one.

His most famous sermon was published under an unlikely title: "The Expulsive Power of a New Affection." In it, he expounded an insight of permanent importance for Christian living: you cannot destroy love for the world merely by showing its emptiness. The world-centered love of our hearts can be expelled only by a new love and affection—for God and from God. The love of the world and the love of the Father cannot coexist in the same heart (1 John 2:15). But the love of the world can be driven out only by the love of the Father. Hence Chalmers' sermon title.

## New Affections

True Christian living, holy and right living, requires a new affection for the Father as its dynamic. Such new affection is part of what William Cowper called "the blessedness I knew when first I saw the Lord"[53]—a love for the holy that seems to deal our carnal affections a deadly blow at the beginning of the Christian life.

Soon, however, we discover that for all that we have died to sin in Jesus Christ (Rom. 6:2), sin has by no means died in us. Sometimes its continued influence surprises us, even appears to overwhelm us in one or another of its manifestations. We discover that our "new affections" for spiritual things must be renewed constantly throughout the whole of our pilgrimage. If we lose our first love, we will find ourselves in serious spiritual peril.

## Substitution no Substitute

Sometimes we make the mistake of substituting other things for new affections. Favorites here are activity and learning. We become active in the service of God ecclesiastically (we gain the positions once held by those we admired and we measure our spiritual growth in terms of position achieved). We become active evangelistically (and in the process measure spiritual strength in terms of increasing influence). Or we become active socially, in moral and political campaigning (and measure growth in terms of involvement).

Alternatively, perhaps we recognize the intellectual fascination and challenge of the gospel and devote ourselves to understanding it, perhaps for its own sake, perhaps to communicate it to others. We measure our spiritual vitality in terms of how articulate we are, even how "correct" our theology is.

But no position, influence, involvement, or correctness can expel love for the world from our hearts. Indeed, they may be expressions of that very love.

Yet others make the mistake of substituting the rules of piety for loving affection for the Father: "Do not touch, do not taste, do not handle" (Col. 2:21). Such disciplines have an air of sanctity about them, but in fact they have no power to restrain the love of the world (cf. Col. 2:20–23). The root of the matter is not on my table or in my neighborhood, but in my heart. Worldliness still has not been expelled.

It is all too possible, in these different ways, to have the form of genuine godliness. But without its power, our subtle hearts are defenseless. Love for the world will not have been expunged, but merely diverted. Only a new love is adequate to expel the old one. Only love for Christ, with all that it implies, can squeeze out the love of this world. Only those who long for

Christ's appearing will be delivered from Demas-like desertion caused by being in love with this world (2 Tim. 4:10).

## *Pathway to Recovery*

How can we recover the new affection for Christ and His kingdom that once so powerfully impacted our lifelong worldliness and caused us to crucify "the flesh with its passions and desires" (Gal. 5:24)?

What was it that created that first love? Do you remember? It was our discovery of Christ's grace in the realization of our own sin.

We are not naturally capable of loving God for Himself; indeed, we hate Him. But in discovering this about ourselves, and in learning of the Lord's supernatural love for us, love for the Father was born. Forgiven much, we loved much (Luke 7:47). We rejoiced in the hope of glory, in suffering, even in God Himself (Rom. 5:2, 3, 11). This new affection seemed first to overtake our worldliness, then to master it. Spiritual realities—Christ, grace, Scripture, prayer, fellowship, service, living for the glory of God—filled our vision and seemed so large, so desirable, that other things by comparison seemed to shrink in size and become bland to the taste.

The way in which we maintain "the expulsive power of a new affection" is the same as the way we first discovered it. Only when grace is still "amazing"—when we return to Christ and the cross where God's love for us was demonstrated to us (Rom. 5:8)—does it retain its power in us. Only as we retain a sense of our own profound sinfulness can we retain a sense of the graciousness of grace.

Many of us share Cowper's sad questions:

*Where is the blessedness I knew,*
*when first I saw the Lord?*
*Where is the soul-refreshing view*
*of Jesus and His Word?*[54]

Let us remember the height from which we have fallen, repent, and return to those first things (Rev. 2:5).

# SABBATH REST

The anonymous author of Hebrews finds different ways of describing the superiority of the Lord Jesus Christ. One of them, which forms the underlying motif of Hebrews 3 and 4, is that Jesus Christ gives the rest that neither Moses nor Joshua could provide.

Under Moses, the people of God were disobedient and failed to enter into God's rest (3:18). In addition, Psalm 95:11 (quoted in Heb. 4:3) implies that Joshua could not have given the people "real rest" since God spoke "through David" about the rest He would give on another day (Heb. 4:7). This in turn implies that "there remains a Sabbath rest for the people of God" (Heb. 4:9, ESV).

In speaking of this rest (3:18; 4:1, 3–6, 8), the author consistently uses the same word (*katapausis*). Then, unexpectedly, he uses a different word in Hebrews 4:9. Here, in speaking about the "rest" that remains for the people of God, he uses the word *sabbatismos*, which appears in the New Testament only here. It means specifically a Sabbath rest.

In the context of Hebrews, this refers fundamentally to the "Sabbath rest" that is found in Christ ("Come . . . I will give you rest," Matt. 11:28–30). Thus, the true-to-Christian-experience paradox of our new life in Christ is that we are to "strive to enter that rest" (4:11, ESV).

Since Augustine, Christians have recognized that the Bible describes human experience in a fourfold scheme: in creation, fall, redemption, and glory.

Many Christians are familiar with echoes of this in the Westminster Confession of Faith, chapter 9, or in Thomas Boston's great book *Human*

*Nature in Its Fourfold State.* It is no surprise, then, that the Sabbath, which was made for man, is experienced by him in four ways.

## Innocence

In Creation, man was made as God's image—intended "naturally," as God's child, to reflect the life and activity of his Father. Since his Father worked creatively for six days and rested on the seventh, Adam, like a son, was to copy Him. On the seventh day, they were to walk together in the garden. That was a time for Adam to listen to all the Father had to show and tell about the wonders of His creating work.

Thus, the Sabbath day was meant to be "Father's Day" every week. It was "made" for Adam. It also had a hint of the future in it. The Father had finished His work, but Adam had not—not yet.

## Fall

Adam fell. He ruined everything, including the Sabbath. Instead of walking with God, he hid from Him (Gen. 3:8). It was the Sabbath, Father's Day, but God had to look for him!

This new context helps us to understand the significance of the fourth commandment in Exodus 20:8. It was given to fallen man—that is why it contains a "you shall not." He was not to work, but to rest. Externally, that meant ceasing from his ordinary tasks in order to meet with God. Internally, it involved ceasing from all self-sufficiency in order to rest in God's grace.

## Salvation

What difference did the coming of Jesus make to the Sabbath day?

In Christ crucified and risen, we find eternal rest (Matt. 11:28–30) and we are restored to communion with God (see Matt. 11:27). The lost treasures of the Sabbath are restored. We rest in Christ from our labor of self-sufficiency and we have access to the Father (Eph. 2:18). As we meet with

Him, He shows us Himself, His ways, His world, His purposes, His glory. And whatever was temporary about the Mosaic Sabbath is left behind as we experience the reality to which it pointed, namely, intimate communion with the risen Savior, free from the pressures of daily work. This is the Lord's Day.

## Glory

But we have not yet reached the goal. We still struggle to rest from the labors of the flesh; we still must "be diligent to enter that rest" (Heb. 4:11). That is why the weekly nature of the Sabbath continues as a reminder that we are not yet home with the Father. And since this rest is ours only through union with Christ in His death and resurrection, our struggles to refuse the old life and enjoy the new will continue until glory.

But one may ask, "How does this impact my Sundays as a Christian?"

For one thing, this view of the Sabbath helps us regulate the whole week. Sunday is "Father's Day," and we have an appointment to meet Him. The child who asks, "How short can the meeting be?" has a dysfunctional relationship problem—not an intellectual, theological problem. Something is amiss in his fellowship with God.

This view of the Lord's Day also usually helps us deal in a non-legalistic way with questions that ask, "Is it OK to do _____ on Sunday since I don't have any time to do it in the rest of the week?" If this is the way we phrase the question, the problem is not how we use Sunday, it is how we are misusing the rest of the week.

This view of the Lord's Day also helps us see it as a foretaste of heaven. And it teaches us that if the worship, fellowship, ministry, and outreach of our churches do not give expression to that, something is seriously amiss.

Hebrews teaches us that eternal glory is a Sabbath rest. Every day, all day, will be "Father's Day"! Thus, if here and now we learn the pleasures of a God-given weekly rhythm, it will no longer seem strange to us that the eternal glory can be described as a prolonged Sabbath!

# CONCLUSION

# IN CHRIST ALONE

The chapters in this book simply "fell into place" one day, just as the names of destinations rearrange themselves on the large "Departures" board in major airports. In a moment in time, *In Christ Alone* was born, complete with title. Or was it meditating on the title that caused the chapters to arrange themselves? I cannot now be sure.

In any event, I am conscious of influences that "triggered" the experience. At the time, I was preaching through John's Gospel during our morning services at First Presbyterian Church in Columbia, S.C. At our Wednesday lunch gatherings, I was expounding the upper room narrative in John 13–17, and on Thursdays at lunch I was engaged in a series on the apostle John himself. It would have been hard not to have been thinking about Christ alone!

But in addition, it was during this period that my longtime friend and colleague Al Groves went to be with Christ. I do not write "to be with Christ" as a euphemism for "death," a way of saying something I would rather avoid saying. No, Al lived in Christ and with Christ. He has simply continued that life now in a new and more glorious way. He knew what Paul was talking about when he said he looked forward to departing (he used the verb that would have been used to speak of a ship slipping her moorings at the beginning of a sea journey). He has gone to be with the Lord, which is better by far (Phil. 1:23).

I am especially grateful for the contact I had with Al during the last year of his life. We had known each other almost exactly twenty-four years, but it was in the last year that I got to know more fully what a heart for Christ he had.

For some reason, I always felt that Al was a little older than I was, but he was actually a few years younger. Perhaps it was because he was a professor of Old Testament—there is something special about learned men of faith who have spent years poring over the Hebrew Bible, reading right to left, absorbing every nuance of meaning. But there was another reason: in grace, faith, and love for Christ, he was an elder brother. It struck me often how well he exemplified Paul's exhortation to Timothy to live so "that your progress may be evident to all" (1 Tim. 4:15). His life was a quiet challenge to students, colleagues, and ministers in whose educating and equipping he had so long shared.

As young men, we joined the faculty at Westminster Theological Seminary in Philadelphia about the same time. We shared the many special blessings of working with men almost twice our age whom we had known first as scholars (and, in Al's case, as teachers) and then had come to love as friends. Those were unique privileges.

Over the years, I watched Al grow steadily in grace. In the end, it flowed from him as if it were natural.

Almost my first impression of Al was how much he loved his wife and then his family, and yet without any of the false Christmas-letter pride of "Aren't we wonderful—can your family match ours?" It was simple, honest, Christ-centered love.

I cherish the email he sent me describing how he sat in his van and watched two students kick a soccer ball around as they waited for others to arrive for a game. Al's description of the choreography was special because one of the students was his elder son and the other was our third son. What was so special was that while he knew that, they didn't. So only later did he learn that, from a distance, he had watched them discover that their fathers were friends and colleagues. I could feel his smile and hear the gentle enthusiasm in his voice as I read his words. It had been a special moment for him to see our lives intertwine again a generation down.

But Al loved and enjoyed his family and friends so much because he enjoyed Christ.

In our last conversations and emails, once inquiries about families had been exchanged, the theme that dominated was just this: Christ alone, and what it means to know and trust Him. To see Al's face crease into a smile as our talk continued was always a sight worth waiting for.

Sometimes Al would tell you how much he had been reflecting on something you had said. But it was obvious when you met face to face that he knew these things already better than you did! That was especially true of our conversations about the experience of Christ's presence.

Here is how his email about our sons continued. The previous May, at the Westminster Seminary commencement, he had given a moving address based on John 15 on the theme of union with Christ. It was a subject we had talked about together, but his address had expressed its grace and wonder in a marvelous way, and I had written a note to thank him. Here is part of his reply:

> Your note to me in June after graduation has been a source of constant meditation and encouragement—grace IN CHRIST, grace from and in the Son of God. All roads lead to him, the mercy we have in him.
>
> God has shown me his grace in Christ in this period more than any period in my life. Our union with Christ, alive forever, has been comforting. Thank you for those words.
>
> This period of life has been a time of continuing to grow in the Lord. God has continued to be a Father, who shows his love by not giving up on the sanctifying process—by which I mean he still disciplines me. Discipline. He never ceases to be a father. Until my final breath, I am learning afresh that I (or anyone else) will never be free of the need to be conformed into the image of our Savior. God still puts his finger on issues in my heart. Instead of despairing, I have learned that it is his great love at work to continue to sanctify. I am grateful; no discipline would mean I am not a son. And, it is far from all discipline!
>
> He has been close at all points. I am a blessed man and have had the gift of time to see his love and blessings through his people. But even better has been the blessing of a constant sense of his presence and comfort. Never have I experienced his closeness as I have in recent months. The word comes alive. I am overwhelmed by his love and find myself often in tears at his love and glory.

There are moments of grief, grief for what I will leave behind, grief that I have been such a blunt instrument in his hand, and yet he has never left nor forsaken me. Grace in Christ. Life through his Spirit indwelling me. There are many moments when I understand so well what Paul says about dying being gain. To see Jesus face to face . . . I do long for that day. There is joy every day as I am able to praise with the breath that I have. So many things seem very different to me.

How do I love as he did?

It did not really surprise me, therefore, when I opened the worship bulletin at Al's memorial service to find two things. The first was the choice of the opening praise: "In Christ Alone." In a few minutes, we would rise to sing the pulsating truths penned by Keith Getty and Stuart Townend:

*In Christ alone my hope is found;*
*He is my light, my strength, my song;*
*This cornerstone, this solid ground,*
*Firm through the fiercest drought and storm.*
*What heights of love, what depths of peace,*
*When fears are stilled, when strivings cease!*
*My comforter, my all in all—*
*Here in the love of Christ I stand.*

How well my friend had experienced that grace and had shown us how to experience the triumph of the final verse:

*No guilt in life, no fear in death—*
*This is the pow'r of Christ in me;*
*From life's first cry to final breath,*
*Jesus commands my destiny.*
*No pow'r of hell, no scheme of man,*
*Can ever pluck me from His hand;*

*Till He returns or calls me home—*
*Here in the pow'r of Christ I'll stand.*

The second thing I found was a letter Al had written for those who attended. Its theme also was "Christ alone." Here are Al's words:

• • •

As I have walked through the valley of the shadow of death, I have walked hand in hand with Jesus, the one who has already walked through that valley and come out the other side, alive, raised from the dead. And as I hold his hand and trust him, I too am raised with him, for this was his purpose in walking that path: to raise those who trusted in him. His rod and staff, his cross of suffering, have become my comfort.

Now as I have died, I come before the God, the king of the universe, and I come in Christ. He chose to suffer and die on the cross in my place, so that on account of him I might have forgiveness from sin and victory over death. And now I have received the resurrection and eternal life that has been my only hope, past, present, and forever.

I have led a truly blessed life. At a young age, I realized that Jesus was not just a story in a comic book, but that he was real and I could actually know him. I wish I could describe to you what a powerful moment of understanding that was, and I have thought about it many times over the years, marveling over and over at the truth of this central fact.

The Lord placed me into the perfect family, where I was raised by loving parents with wonderful siblings. God gave me a wonderful wife who has been my joy as we have raised four wonderful children together. The Lord has given me the opportunity to be intimately involved in the lives of so many wonderful brothers and sisters, in our fellowship at college, as a pastor in Vermont, as an elder at New Life Church, and as a professor at Westminster Seminary. Through family and ministry, I have had the privilege of loving and being loved by all of you, and I have been struck again and again by the deposit that each of you has left in my life.

Through all my life, Christ has been constant. Even as I have grown and changed, he is still the one whom I loved that first day. And nothing ever changed in how I came to him; every day of my life the story is the same: I come to God in Christ. His love for me has been steadfast, and he has pursued me through every time I have turned away from him and every time I have returned. The constant prayer of my heart for my own life and the lives of those around me has been that we would see Jesus, and that he would be welcome and present among us.

There may be some here who have never trusted Christ for life, who have never known that he is the answer to the sin and death in our lives. I urge you to consider the claims he made to being the Son of God, to consider that he didn't stay dead and sends a message down through the ages that there is life in him and him alone. His death on a cross, humiliating though it seemed, was his glory, by which he has defeated our true enemies—sin and death. By the ultimate sacrifice he made, he humiliated all powers arrayed against him.

If you struggle with faith, let me encourage you that in the hardest moments I have faced, he has been there. And death has been defeated. I am in Christ, as you are in Christ. So let us live out of the grace we have received. Let us live out of Christ. This means looking daily for him, asking him to open your eyes to him, and embracing what you see.

Seek him with all your heart. Love him with all your heart. Love those he loves with all your heart, even to the laying down of your life for him. Jesus, the way, the truth, the life. In no other do we have hope. But in him we have hope that endures forever. We grieve, but we grieve with hope. The hope of a resurrection; the hope of life eternal. Together with Jesus.

For most of my Christian life I have wanted to see Jesus face to face, to join in with the heavenly chorus in his presence around his royal throne and declare his praise in new ways. Something else has grown through the years: an abiding sense that this is not for me alone. Being with Jesus by myself is not what he wants, nor is it what I want. To be there with you all, those he loves and those I have come to love, that is true joy. I have often thought of coming to heaven as Jesus standing at the finish line of a race awaiting those looking for him, trusting in him, pursuing him. But it isn't a race for me to finish first or alone. It has always been a race for us to finish together, arm in arm, having encouraged one another in faith.

He is good. From the beginning, his steadfast love has endured. It endures forever. He is a gracious God, slow to anger, abounding in steadfast love. Trust in him with all your heart, for he is faithful.

• • •

This is the message of *In Christ Alone*. The book might well have had the same title even apart from Al's influence. It is, after all, a watchword used to describe the gospel rediscovered by the Reformers in the sixteenth century. But I am thankful that its publication now has caused me to reflect on the last twenty-five years of God's grace to me, and especially of the friendships with which He has so richly blessed me on the way.

Truly to live in Christ alone is God's way of life for us. My prayer is that these reflections on that life may be a help and an encouragement to you, too, to live *In Christ Alone*.

# NOTES

1   These lines represent, in poetic form, a truly magnificent paragraph about the riches that are ours in Christ alone. They are found in John Calvin's *Institutes of the Christian Religion,* II.16.19. Neither the title nor the versification is Calvin's. Though I am neither a gifted poet nor translator, these lines give expression to my personal meditative understanding of Calvin's Latin.

2   John Calvin, *The Gospel According to John,* trans. T. H. L. Parker, eds. D. W. and T. F. Torrance (Edinburgh: Oliver and Boyd, 1959), 1, 6.

3   Ibid., 20.

4   Isaiah's vivid language would more literally be translated "a garment of menstruation."

5   From the hymn "Who Is He in Yonder Stall?" by Benjamin R. Hanby, 1866.

6   B. B. Warfield, *Selected Shorter Writings,* ed. J. E. Meeter (Nutley, N.J.: Presbyterian & Reformed, 1970), 1, 153.

7   Arianism was so called after its leading proponent, Arius of Alexandria (c. 250–336), who rejected the idea that the Son of God was without beginning. The controversy that followed was formally settled at the Council of Nicaea in AD 325 by the affirmation that the Son was *homoousios* (of one and the same substance) with the Father, not *homoiousios* (of like substance). The Arian view has erupted from time to time in the history of the church ever since.

8   From the hymn "Christ the Lord Is Risen Today" by Charles Wesley, 1739.

9   J. N. D. Kelly, *A Commentary on the Epistles of Peter and of Jude* (London: A&C Black, 1969), 206.

10  From Luther's comments on Romans in his Preface to his German translation of the Bible (1522).

11  The noun was used in secular Greek especially of the exchange of money.

12  Calvin, *Institutes of the Christian Religion,* III.1.1.

13  Cited by J. R. W. Stott in *The Cross of Christ* (Leicester: InterVarsity Press, 1986), 197.

14  B. B. Warfield, *Biblical and Theological Studies* (Philadelphia: Presbyterian and Reformed, 1952), 425.

15  Martin Luther, *Lectures on Romans,* trans. and ed. W. Pauck (London and Philadelphia: S.C.M. Press and Westminster Press, 1961), 3–4.

16  It seems that the practice of wrapping cloths around a newborn infant was rooted in the belief that thus restricting the baby's movements would prevent him or her

from developing physical problems in the limbs later in life. To this extent, our Lord was subjected to the ignorance of Mary and Joseph, who, clearly, loved Him dearly.

17  From the hymn "Jesus, I My Cross Have Taken" by Henry F. Lyte, 1824.

18  Gregory of Nyssa, his brother Basil the Great, and his close friend Gregory Nazianzus formed a small group of influential leaders usually known as the Cappadocian fathers, who staunchly defended the orthodox doctrine of the Trinity.

19  From the hymn "Love Divine, All Loves Excelling" by Charles Wesley, 1747.

20  Jonathan Edwards, *A History of the Work of Redemption,* in *The Works of Jonathan Edwards*, 2 vols. (Edinburgh: Banner of Truth Trust, 1974 reprint), 1:539.

21  *The Memoir and Remains of Robert Murray McCheyne*, ed. Andrew Bonar (Edinburgh: Banner of Truth Trust, 1966; first published 1844, expanded 1892), 93.

22  From the hymn "When I Survey the Wondrous Cross" by Isaac Watts, 1707.

23  B. B. Warfield, *Calvin and Calvinism*, in *The Works of Benjamin B. Warfield*, 10 vols. (New York: Oxford University Press, 1932), 5:21.

24  John Owen, *Works, Vol. 4*, ed. W. H. Goold (Edinburgh: Johnstone and Hunter, 1850–1853; Edinburgh and London: Banner of Truth Trust, 1967), 475.

25  John Murray, *Collected Writings* (Edinburgh: Banner of Truth Trust, 1976), 1.188.

26  From the hymn "Christ the Lord Is Risen Today" by Charles Wesley, 1739.

27  From the hymn "Ah, Dearest Jesus" by Martin Luther, 1535 (translated by Catherine Winkworth).

28  From the hymn "Jesus, I My Cross Have Taken" by Henry F. Lyte, 1824.

29  From the hymn "Rock of Ages, Cleft for Me" by Augustus M. Toplady, 1776.

30  T. S. Eliot, opening lines of "Burnt Norton," in *The Four Quartets* (London: Faber and Faber, 1959).

31  Martin Luther, *Luther's Works, Vol. 35*, eds. Jaroslav J. Pelikan and Helmut T. Lehmann (Philadelphia: Fortress Press, 1960), 370

32  From the hymn "Trust and Obey" by John H. Sammis, 1887.

33  Charles H. Spurgeon, "The Last Words of Christ," in *The Metropolitan Tabernacle Pulpit, Vol. 45* (London: Passmore and Alabaster, 1899), 495.

34  Calvin, *Institutes of the Christian Religion*, III.20.4.

35  Ibid., III.20.7

36  John Owen, *Works, Vol. 6*, ed. W. H. Goold (Edinburgh: Johnstone and Hunter, 1850–1853; Edinburgh and London: Banner of Truth Trust, 1966), 300.

37  Ibid., 299.

38  John Flavel, "Navigation Spiritualized," in *The Works of John Flavel, Vol. 5* (Edinburgh: Banner of Truth Trust, 1968), 284.

39  From the hymn "God Moves in a Mysterious Way" by William Cowper, 1774.

40  Calvin, *Institutes of the Christian Religion*, III.19.11.

41  Martin Luther, "Treatise on Christian Liberty," in *Three Treatises*, trans. W. A. Lambert and H. J. Grimm (Philadelphia: Fortress Press, 1970), 261.

42  Alexander Smellie, *Robert Murray McCheyne* (London: National Council of Free Evangelical Churches, 1913), 203–204.

43  Samuel Rutherford, *Letters of Samuel Rutherford*, ed. Andrew Bonar (Edinburgh: Banner of Truth Trust, 1984; first printed 1891), 148.

44  From the hymn "Father, I Know that All My Life" by Anna L. Waring, 1850.

45  First published in 1648 and still in print today.

46  *The Memoir and Remains of Robert Murray McCheyne*, 34.

47  William Still (1911–1997) was minister of Gilcomston South Church, Aberdeen, from 1945–1997 and a significant figure in the emergence of biblical, expository preaching in the second half of the twentieth century.

48  From the hymn "Approach, My Soul, the Mercy Seat" by John Newton, 1779.

49  Ibid.

50  Amy Carmichael of Donhavur, India (1867–1951).

51  *The Memoir and Remains of Robert Murray McCheyne*, 153.

52  Charles Simeon (1759–1836) was one of the most influential ministers in the history of evangelicalism in the Church of England, especially in promoting biblical exposition. He ministered at Holy Trinity Church, Cambridge, for more than half a century and befriended and helped a great number of students, including the brilliant young Henry Martyn (1781–1812), who, among other things, by the time of his early death had translated the New Testament into Urdu, Persian, and Arabic. Simeon kept a portrait of him as a reminder of his zeal for Christ.

53  From the hymn "O for a Closer Walk with God" by William Cowper, 1772.

54  Ibid.

# About the Author

D r. Sinclair B. Ferguson is senior minister of the historic First Presbyterian Church in Columbia, S.C., and a distinguished visiting professor of systematic theology at Westminster Theological Seminary in Dallas, Texas.

A native of Scotland, Dr. Ferguson earned three degrees, including his Ph.D., from the University of Aberdeen. He was ordained into the ministry in the Church of Scotland and spent some sixteen years in ministry in his homeland, including five years at St. George's Tron Church in Glasgow.

Dr. Ferguson has served as a professor of systematic theology at Westminster Theological Seminary's campuses in Philadelphia and in Dallas, as well as at other U.S. seminaries.

He has been an editor and a trustee with the Banner of Truth Trust publishing house and has been a prolific author. His published titles include *The Holy Spirit, Grow in Grace, Let's Study Philippians, John Owen on the Christian Life,* and, for children, *The Big Book of Questions & Answers* and *The Big Book of Questions & Answers About Jesus.*

Dr. Ferguson is a member of the council of the Alliance of Confessing Evangelicals and has spoken at the annual Alliance-sponsored Philadelphia Conference on Reformed Theology, as well as the annual Ligonier Ministries National Conference.

Dr. Ferguson and his wife, Dorothy, have been married for thirty-six years. They have four children.